This edition is
a mock-up only,
still fixing typos,
pagination and
lay-out!

(Review copy/returned)

Fringe

By Jaima Chevalier

Printed in the United States of America.

First printing, June 2019.
ISBN: 978-1-68184-241-7

Atomic City Lights Publishers
2384 35th Street
Los Alamos, NM 87544-2004
Email: PictureThisNewMexico@icloud.com
(505) 982-0929

Cover Image: Ruven Afanador
Back Page Image: Winter Prather, Image courtesy Winter Prather Collection (Ph.00332), History Colorado

Graphic Design:
Emilee Rae Jones

Library of Congress
Cataloging-in-Publication
Data on file

DEDICATION

María Benítez's devotion to her husband, Cecilio, was a character trait that defied her artistic reputation as a fiery soloist who did not need the trappings of a conventional domestic life to survive. Although hers is indeed a singular life story, no retelling of it is complete without the understanding that she was part of a team that she loved fiercely: her husband and her son, Francisco ("Paco") Benítez as well as Paco's wife, Anne, and Cecilio's son José María Benítez de Sande and daughter Afriquita Carrasco Benítez. Lastly, María's story is one link in the chain of students and teachers of dance circling back in time, from yesterday, through today, and on to tomorrow.

TABLE OF CONTENTS

AT THE BEGINNING

On April 19, 1993, *New York Daily News* described María Benítez's dance form as representative of a full-flowered talent in perfect command of the stage: "Her long, elegant fingers uncurl like petals opening; her back is straight; her head high; her feet command the floor to release sounds that range from seductive taps to angry thunder." Although it might have seemed like she had burst onto the scene fully-formed, her back story is where María's true greatness is revealed, and that is what we set forth here in this compendium of photographs and accompanying essay. Understanding her perfect choreography, carriage, or beauty is a superficial glance upon the surface of very deep waters. We analyze how María rose from improbable circumstances to become the doyenne of American flamenco, and despite her grand success, how she fought to bring young people up onto the stage. She accomplished this by making her instructional methods widely accepted, and by finding a place for the Spanish arts in school curricula throughout the country, thereby influencing succeeding generations, and building her dance legacy as much through education as she did through performance. With this intent, María spent decades performing

and teaching wherever and whenever she could, in almost a subversive or secret way of forcing flamenco into the mainstream: taking it from the fringe or outskirts to the center stage. Her rigid devotion to teaching is what constitutes her greatest gift to her adopted state of New Mexico, and from there to grander stages around the world.

During her long professional career, María spoke through footfalls and body language and gestures as much as she did through words. But she was not just a staged flashpoint, orchestrated for a raw reaction or a base reflex. She was equally eloquent off-stage as on, and in every setting her personal story came through with a deep clang, like a deliberate message from an ancient bell. Something that you understood intrinsically, and something that you craved to hear again and again and again.

Her dance was the same way. The choreography spoke in a measured way, despite the body movements twisting this way and that; despite being uncontainable—almost indescribable—the purpose was evident. The Andalusian Roma (gypsies) of southern Spain are closely identified with flamenco, and it was on Spanish soil that the Roma intermingled with the Sephardic Jews and the Moors. This complicated turf was not unlike the complex landscape of New Mexico, where this biography is primarily rooted.

María compared the evolution of flamenco to the evolution of jazz; both art forms borne of persecuted people and with similar construction: the theme is introduced and then riffs are explored by the performers in

a type of improvisation that is almost impossible to trademark. Both jazz and flamenco contain the element of surprise, which María describes as "tension and quietness" driven by "fire and passion." Each pattern builds upon the immediate past, trailing the memory of what you had just seen or heard and forecasting the next spiral of thinking ahead: like a murmuration of silent birds, her movements swelled in patterns that ebbed and flowed, receded and drew close, rising to a crescendo like an avian ballet, all pointed with some purpose in a communal mind, where everything is connected, even if it seems disjointed and free. Just when it might seem possible to predict where she was going, she could rear up and upend all expectations. Upside down and back to the front, she extruded raw emotion out of her soul to flog the audience into recognition of the profound. She wanted you to see her internal viscera more than her exterior.

When María's image exploded on the cover of *Dance Magazine* in 1984, she was trying single-handedly to change the American dance vernacular. It was akin to a door slamming shut inexplicably in the middle of the night. The force that had propelled this exotic art form to the front and center was demanding your attention.

Although the clichés of "new" and "fresh" are suitably apt to describe María's talents, these adjectives fail miserably to evoke the mysterious quality of her choreography that was born from something very old and very dark. In the primal deep of ancestral memory where the anvil clanged or the stone struck an iron bell or a plaintive voice called workers to the field, María

Dance Magazine

NOVEMBER 1984

$2.75

SPANISH FLAME MARIA BENITEZ!

BRUHN'S NEW EMPIRE: THE NATIONAL BALLET OF CANADA

YOKO ICHINO

TORONTO'S NATIONAL BALLET SCHOOL

BARYSHNIKOV: THE RUSSIAN YEARS

CHRISTMAS GIFT-GIVING WITH STYLE

733616   11

Maria Benitez
Estampa Flamenca!

by Joan Pikula   *photos by Jack Mitchell*

Considered one of the greatest flamenco dancers of our time, Benitez captivates audiences with her stunning heelwork and subtle, smoldering interpretation of the Spanish dance idioms. What she has is duende—*the "dark soul" from which all true flamenco springs.*

Maria Benitez, who has been hailed as the "Baryshnikov of Spanish dance" in the *Boston Globe* and the "Makarova of flamenco" in the *San Francisco Examiner*, has been barnstorming around the country since early September with her Estampa Flamenca, gleaning a new batch of rave reviews. In fact, she's been on this kind of whistle-stop touring routine since 1972 when she formed her company. And everywhere, from the *New York Times* to the *Village Voice* to *Variety* to the *Denver Post* and the *Rocky Mountain News*, she has been praised for her "crackling display of temperament and discipline," "her coiled energy and sensuous vibrancy," and called "a phenomenon," a "living legend of Spanish dance," a "brilliant virtuoso."

Clearly a Spanish dancer of extraordinary talent, Maria Benitez is an American.

She was born in the Cass Lake Indian Hospital in Minnesota, the daughter of a Chippewa-Oneida Indian mother and a Puerto Rican father—Geraldine and Josue Elm Diaz. They named their daughter Maria Woosha—Woosha, "Girl Bringer of Happiness."

At ten, Maria and her family moved to Taos, and the child grew in the hot, dry climate of New Mexico, surrounded by the ancient Pueblo village of San Geronimo de Taos on the north, the old Spanish farming center of Ranchos de Taos on the south, and the Sangre de Cristo Mountains looming above. She studied piano. And she studied dance—not Spanish, but classical ballet (her teachers over the years would include Jacques Cartier, Louise Locklear, Igor Schwezoff, and Francesca Romanoff). Then one day a friend gave her a lesson in Spanish dance. That day she found her métier.

She went to Spain at nineteen to study dance. There, for five years, she learned and she performed, touring as soloist and principal dancer with the Maria Rosa and Paquita Rico companies, and dancing in small flamenco groups as well. "I studied hard when I went to Spain," she recalls, "and I got into a company after six months—which is no big deal; there are a lot of companies in Spain, a lot of working opportunities."

Currently on tour throughout the United States, Maria Benitez, seen at left in her Soleà and at right in an alegrìas, will dedicate her November 27–December 1 season at the Joyce Theatre in New York City to the legendary Spanish dancer José Greco—who will perform as a guest.

DANCEMAGAZINE November 1984

owned the universe of history. Flamenco dancers of old had told these stories by campfires on the fringes of towns or in immigrant camps, wandering without nation or tribe, but always with purpose. As borders around nations changed and governments rose and fell, the histories carried forth in the world did not fade away. But María brought something more to the stage, something of her own inner personal history. She occupied an equipoise between the human tradition of storytelling through movement versus the flash of insight that occurs when the self is given up to the divine. Somehow what was transmitted to the viewer was something intensely personal and also sacred, not mindless parable or hackneyed soap opera. Her dance story did not talk down to the audience, she expected the audience to listen and to understand, but, most importantly, she wanted the audience to *feel*.

This command of the stage was a kind of universal tuning fork; somehow gathering up all the emotions ever felt in dance and transmitting them wholesale, like an arrow shot from a full quiver straight to a quivering carcass— an instantaneous death of what was once known in exchange for a new understanding of what will be. In a way that a cleric might attend to duties on an altar before an assembly, María operated in her own world, completely focused on a personal communion that no third party could breach despite their presence in the room. The act performed takes place in existing light, not spotlighted like a performance, so although the congregants comprise an audience, they know they are supposed to participate in the act of worship—not entertainment—

and to follow the dictates of the ceremony. Only the mediator can call forth the spirit or send up the prayer. María's legion of fans often touch on this dynamic; describing how her presence on

the stage was the only time her character came through, and how they felt privy to some private supplication. It was when she was performing that a priestess was revealed, bringing godliness to the fore with spiritual fervor.

Attending María's performances was to witness absorption into the divine, a religious experience of sorts. She could include the audience in a communal experience that she beamed outward in all directions in a dragonfly or "Pueblo Cross" manner. The dragonfly is capable of six directions, plus the ability to hover in place like a helicopter, making this insect capable of seven states of being: the four directions, up and down, and centered. During this "centering" state that María possessed, she could

absorb immediate audience reaction to the dance and then simultaneously rebroadcast that to everyone there. Even though she was playing a role that required adherence to a certain part or story, she chose to also assume a separate role of conducting the entire proceedings. Holding these two roles of performer and director concurrently gave María a state of being while not being. Occupying these different spaces on the stage with undetectable transitions made for a quantum rush experience when the audience knew something had just happened, even if they weren't sure exactly how to explain it.

This book will present a vast range of images of María that not only speak to her incredible form and precision, but are testament to the fact that she created a vernacular all her own, and that she left a story in her thundering wake that escapes the confines of page or border and instead speaks in subliminal ways, and in memory. The text is augmented by exclusive images curated

with an eye to bottling this elusive elixir. María loathes the adjective "exotic"—preferring instead to be understood and accessible across both the external geography of the world but also throughout internal cultures not confined to place; such as realms of the nomadic *gitano*, Jewish mysticism, Arabic poetry, cinematic cultures such as Bollywood—as well as María's own heritage borne of both Native American and Hispanic diasporas—these were her secret worlds that she carried within her soul so that she might cross-pollinate with other souls or populate new places in the heart.

While her stature as an *impresaria* of flamenco is well-established, María's character and personal inner backstory are somewhat elusive. Maintaining an air of mystery—the refusal to divulge the routine facts of her existence—was what set her apart. Her full biography is a volume for another day. For now, we present an impressionistic sketch of a sage, an actress, a beauty, and an empress who served as a lit fuse for all of the emotional intensity of flamenco. Her trademarks were muscle and shine and fear and spine.

Sometimes her dancing was
difficult to watch because it was
akin to prying into personal
trauma and anguish. She could
appear to be so angular that it
looked like bone would pierce
her skin at any moment, or so
fluid that the bones seemed
to disappear altogether. This
ability to transcend the physical
form was María's strong suit;
she took up residency in a kind
of "between" place where
interstitial spokes are the
superstructure for everything
mysterious. She was and is
an elusive
enigma—
like that
murmuration
swelling in the
phenomenon
known as The
Black Sun—
when all the
birds in a cluster
rise to blot out
the sun. María's
storytelling bore
an intelligence
that seemed
to be about
something so
important that
it flew right into
the main power source in order
to extinguish it completely.

PREFACE

In assisting María on her long over-due memoir, it became clear to me that the material transcended a standard autobiographical or biographical format. Given the profound impact her dancing had on the art of flamenco in general, and on audiences in particular, any record of her life needs to resonate from more than just her recollections; it percolates up from a deep well of the memories of people that she affected, and her legacy of dance instruction in New Mexico, and, in some ways, from the long tortured history of the confluence of Indigenous America and the Spanish who conquered the area—a past that is reflected everywhere in the state, with ripples throughout the American Southwest and beyond. This grand and timeless story erupted, in singular fashion, through the choreography and aesthetic of María's dance legacy. The goal, then, was to capture an evocative portrait of an extraordinary figure in American dance, but also one who figured into the everyday lives of New Mexicans as well and made a lasting impact on the state's culture.

There are few places in the world where it can be said that the landscape forms the person. New Mexico is one of those places.

Much as Georgia O'Keeffe's career did not reach its zenith until she painted New Mexico, the same can be said of María Benítez's career. Something about the grandeur and the privations, the isolation and the desolation, and the stark beauty of the land and sky and people are inexplicably linked with the form of flamenco that María brought to the forefront in New Mexico. Further, the unique cultural and social makeup of the state has endowed its people with the ability to lay claim to art forms that originated elsewhere. As soon as an art form is adapted to the rough landscape and myriad of cultures of the state, that art form morphs into something uniquely identified with The Land of Enchantment.

Given the context of the communal belief that María's legend blossomed on New Mexican soil, we tell the story of her life and career from the well-spring of the state's own profound origin story. This nexus between place and person produces a compelling story, beginning with her own authentic voice, augmented by voices from the past, and finally with stellar photographs that form a curved trajectory across the world stage. And this portrait is an arc of sorts for the story of New Mexico as well, a place where the land itself embodies spirit.

In this volume, we also explore the question of whether or not—or even how—Native American belief systems or ideology informed María's character or her choreography. In matriarchal societies, the female holds predominance in certain spheres of life. In some clan systems, women and mothers are the "house." In Navajo and other cultures, the changing woman is a core belief. Gender roles are part and parcel of the Native world. María was raised primarily by her mother, so we explore how this fact and the tension between her tribal and Spanish heritage made her the ultimate outsider—to her advantage.

Many of the images in this book have been arduously collected over many years, so we are profoundly grateful for each and every donation, permission, and contribution. With a list of contributors that reads like a "who's who" of famous photographers, including Ruven Afanador, Winter Prather, Robin Holland, Don J. Usner, Morgan Smith, Lois Greenfield, Jack Mitchell, Ken Howard, Brian Fishbine, Beverly Gile, and many others, the lush visuals of María's striking face and physique are classic iconic images that capture the movement and feeling that she embodied. Artist Jo Ann Garcia Orellana, who at one time ran the box office for María, created the stunning collage for the book.

A word about pronouns: we use the given name "María" herein because, although it is not journalistically proper, it accurately captures how everyone addressed her—by her first name—the archetypal, the original, the one-and-only María. We chose first person in lieu of the more formal "Benítez" simply because it not only suits her, but her persona has that biblical primacy of the first Rebecca or Ezekiel, the archetypal Moses or Cain. As tribute to her singular firebrand, she is and was María. In ways that we will describe later, New Mexico also came to declare María as an original native New Mexican, despite the fact that her birthplace was elsewhere.

The book's structure is non-linear in order to focus on Benítez' extraordinary path as a feminist who was driven to forge her own way in the world by starting a business, a non-profit institution, a school, and a professional touring company. Given New Mexico's new-found international renown as a national, if not world center for flamenco, María's history of establishing programs for the Spanish arts—not just dance but guitar and theater and poetry and song—provides a detailed conclusion about her lasting contributions to the state's culture, education, and arts. The deep meaning of her choreography and legacy are the "through threads" that make the book structure the right frame for the facts of her life. Her ability to overcome both racial and gender discrimination and to move in royal circles across Europe— equally comfortable on the stage of the Metropolitan Opera as she was dancing before a gypsy campfire—all coalesce to make her story one that dances straight into the heart of what it means to be an American original.

ACKNOWLEDGEMENTS

So many New Mexicans and other people scattered across the globe assisted us in this endeavor that it is impossible to thank everyone, but to highlight a few we must extend our profound gratitude to the following:

Francisco Benítez
Jo Ann Garcia Orellana
Rebecca Avitia
Valerie Martinez
Robin Farwell Gavin
Valerie Rangel
Ken Howard
Tom Maguire
Maria Montez Skolnick
Deirdre Towers
Marisa Xochtl Jimenez
Gomeo Bobelu
Anna Maria Chavez
Morgan Smith

The author owes a huge debt to Lea Ann Boone, for her bravery battling the "word clouds" at the same time that she was facing skirmishes of her own in a faraway land.

CHAPTER ONE - THE EMERGENCE PLACE

Duende is a Spanish word capable of many meanings, but with only one measurement—either you have it or you don't. If your entire being beats intuitively to an indescribable feeling colored by the sights and sounds of Andalucía, or if the passion and inspiration of flamenco awakens knowledge of its unfathomable story in your heart, then you have *duende*. There was never a doubt about María— she was born with *duende*, and she personified it completely.

"Belonging" is not a word in the lexicon of words that might be used to describe María. She did not personify the sense that she craved belonging. She evoked almost a disdain for needy or weak things. María shunned cloying sweetness or overt familiarity, especially if it was feigned. She eschewed clubs and cliques and groups. She was a lonely only child raised here and there in the great American West by her Native American mother, moving from one academic post to another, sometimes on Indian land, sometimes not. María certainly didn't pick a popular or mainstream dance form to study, and when she sojourned off to faraway Spain to learn everything that she could about an art form mostly alien to America, this singularity of purpose transformed her into almost a personification of the absence of belonging, giving off the manner of a person perhaps otherworldly. María took up a defiant residency on the fringe or outskirts of life and conventionality and culture, at times even defying the strictures of gender, race, and place of origin. This mindset of hers brings us to one of the most crucial aspects of her origin story: the fact that it was manufactured in a way to give her a cachet that she wanted, while at the same time giving her the authenticity that she decidedly deserved.

Native American origin stories, especially in the Southwest, are often associated with a creation ideology that begins in underworlds, places from which a people emerge to arrive in this world above. For example, the Zuni people emerge from the Fourth Underworld to the Grand Canyon. Indigenous history cannot be described by the use of artificial borders applied to the map by others. María's story is likewise not pegged to a point on a map; rather, it is somehow part of the story of the Indigenous people of New Mexico: beginning at a place of emergence, followed by a migration story. María's own place of emergence was not Taos Pueblo as is commonly presumed. Instead, her improbable origin story defies

Images of Geraldine DeCoteau Harvey, María's mother

Western civilization's use of lines, points, miles and markers. Her origin story breaks free from the map to how a Native/Puerto Rican child of modest means raised in a dusty outpost of New Mexico rose to become a doyenne of the flamenco world.

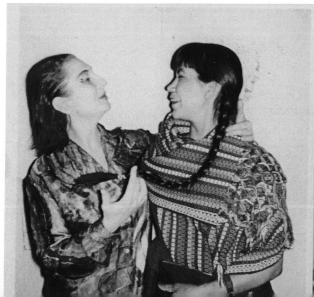

"Taos Maiden", circa 1905. Photo by B.G. Randall, (c) 1987 Las Quince Letras.

Although the major myth of María's life is that everyone believes that she was born in Taos Pueblo, or at least in the town of Taos, or certainly somewhere in New Mexico, those are not the facts of her origin. The truth of her story is deeper, and more interesting, and it begins with her mother. María's mother, Geraldine DeCoteau Díaz, née Harvey, was born in Wisconsin. Her paternal heritage was Chippewa and Algonquin, and her maternal heritage was Oneida and Iroquois. Some Ojibwe heritage was also part of her lineage. She was the first Native American woman to earn a master's degree in education from the University of Wisconsin. In South Dakota she met her future husband, Josué Eliu Díaz, who was from Puerto Rico. Their only child, María Woesha Díaz,

was born in Cass County, Minnesota on April 14, 1942, near Leech Lake and the Chippewa National Forest.

After separation from María's father, Harvey travelled around the American West as an itinerant scholar and teacher, frequently teaching elementary school in isolated areas. She taught the Menominee in Wisconsin, the Sioux in Montana, and the Apaches in Oklahoma. She also taught the Cheyenne and the Blackfoot before finally ending up in Taos, New Mexico, not in the Pueblo as is commonly believed, but on the outskirts, where she remained for over fifty years.

María's formative years had to have been colored by the ever-changing cultures that she was exposed to due to her constant address changes. María owed her heritage to indigenous peoples from the northern part of the American continent, and grew up around Plains and Pueblo Indians. The belief systems of these various indigenous groups are very

different from each other. There is no monolithic belief system or people. Understanding this framework helps us to understand how María essentially constructed her own personal origin story and mythology, cobbling together concepts from the range of cultures she descended from, but also from the cultures that she observed around her. She was mostly raised in isolated tribal communities before moving to Taos, where Pueblo and Spanish culture dominated. At the time of María's arrival in Taos, the sleepy settlement was a dusty village about an hour and half north of Santa Fé, perched near the dramatic Rio Grande Gorge and beneath the Taos mountains and glittering Blue Lake. But Taos has a complex cultural history which weaves together strands from many cultures: Pueblo, Spanish, the Old West, and, in the early 20th century before María and her mother arrived, a new identity as an artist colony.

"Taos Intertribal Dance" circa 1905, photo by B.G.Randall, postcard (c) 1987 Las Quince Letras.

Taos Silhouette, circa 1905. Photo by B. G. Randall, Postcard (c) 1987 Las Quince Letras.

Taos is an extraordinary place, an area defined by its geography, its history, and the gradual mixing of cultures from that history. The area was first inhabited perhaps 11,000 years ago or more, and by about 1000 CE, the pueblo culture, an indigenous way of life associated with groups of multi-story dwellings, stretched throughout what is now New Mexico. Taos Pueblo was built sometime between 1000 and 1400 CE. Spanish explorers appeared about 1540, and soon the conquistador armies arrived. In 1598, Don Juan de Oñate declared sovereignty over the area. After the conquest, however, tensions remained between the Pueblos and the colonists, who enslaved the Natives, and also the Spanish missionary priests, who attempted to suppress Native religious practices. Taos Pueblo revolted in 1640, although Spanish rule was soon re-established. In 1680, the Pueblos of the region united under the leadership of Po'pay, from Ohkay Owingeh, and revolted against the Spanish, who then fled southward to El Paso. In 1692, the Spanish began a campaign to retake the Pueblos. In 1692 and again in 1693, Don Diego de Vargas re-conquered Ogapogeh, "White Shell Water Place," the ancient name the Native Americans had given to the area that later became Santa Fé. The conquest was completed in Taos in 1696. In the late 1700s, the Spanish gave land grants to many Spanish families in the Taos Valley, and the settlement of Taos was established close to Taos Pueblo.

The mixing of Spanish and Native cultures was not a straightforward combination. Many aspects of Native culture persisted, but turned to secrecy in practice. One aspect of this hiddenness is the role that privacy played in religion. The kiva, an underground structure, had long been the center of Pueblo religion, and its rituals were closely guarded, but the rule of the Spanish meant that these religious practices became even more hidden. For example, the Spanish were known to fill the kivas with sand to prevent their use, and sacred icons were destroyed, replaced by the cross.

Nor was the Native religion the only practice that was conducted in secret. It is perhaps not well-known that Don Juan de Oñate's colonists included many Jewish settlers. These settlers did not openly identify as Jews—a

"Plains Dance" in Taos, circa 1905. Photo by B.G. Randall, (c) 1987 Las Quince Letras.

María and her mother emerging from a kiva in New Mexico. Photography of these sacred places is not allowed unless the governing pueblo has deconsecrated the structure, or has erected one for tourism purposes.

royal edict in 1492 had required all Spaniards to either accept Christianity by being baptized or face forfeiture of their property and expulsion from Spain. But even though they were nominally Catholics, these *conversos* brought their own worship and traditions to the New World, continuing to practice in secret. In later years, further secretive religious practices developed in the Catholic faith in the region. When the Spanish left the colony after Mexican independence in 1821, their priests followed. An unofficial priesthood and lay ministry, the *penitentes* and the *hermanidad*, grew up to fill the void left by the loss of Catholic hierarchy. These unofficial priests practiced their religion in secret meeting places called *moradas*, where unique Catholic traditions were preserved, although they

had been prohibited initially by the Catholic bureaucracy. These complex circumstances meant that much of religious life in New Mexico was practiced in secret, most notably for Indigenous people, Jewish *conversos*, and at times, even those of Catholic faith. *Kivas* and *moradas* were a way of life in the dusty realm.

María and her mother thus arrived in a place that already had a mix of Native and Spanish culture. However, as far as tribal membership was concerned, María did not fit in. Membership in the Native community of the Pueblo is restricted primarily to those of Tiwa heritage. Taos Hispanics are also decidedly a

breed apart, and occupied a world that María could not easily penetrate given the fact that her Hispanic heritage was from Puerto Rico—making her unlike the special blend of Spanish heritage found in northern New Mexico, where even the spoken Spanish is quite different from elsewhere. María did not learn much Spanish from her mother, so the fact that she later became proficient at it is a testament to her sheer will power and determination.

María says, "Of course I think about my childhood, and the most distinct thing in my mind in my memories of living on Indian reservations was that I was always confused—very confused—as to where I stood within the Indian community; mostly because we didn't speak the right language. Unfortunately, my mother wasn't able to learn anything but English because she went to state boarding schools when she was a child." Her mother's parents were from different tribes and as a consequence mostly used English at home; additionally, her mother

Image of Taos Fair during Territorial days, circa 1905. Image by B.G. Randall. (c) 1986 Las Quince Letras.

María and her posse voguing as Western varmints

spent about 30 years working with the Bureau of Indian Affairs mostly on Indian reservations in the American West where the languages were unfamiliar. María continues, "Naturally I didn't speak any of these languages, so consequently I fall rather as an outsider with tribal people. And it was also because of the [Spanish] language that I never felt that I totally bonded with my Puerto Rican father. I didn't learn Spanish from him either because my parents were divorced when I was very small, so I lost out on three languages right there. And as far as Spanish dance: I wanted to become a dancer. I remember knowing that a long time ago, starting when I was about 10, and I think by 12, I was beginning to see clearly that dance was the thing I wanted to do."

Even as some aspects of this rich mix of cultures

in New Mexico remained hidden, various groups have long interacted openly—in trade, in conflict, and in searches for opportunity, adventure, and, later, artistic self-transformation. In ancient times, Natives traded at the intersection of various trails near Taos. Parrot feathers from Mexico might be bartered in exchange for pelts from Apache people from the Plains. These active trade trails and cultural exchanges informed the art and utility of everyday life. Given the web of trails and by-ways of the state, as well as its stature as a grand stage for epic battles, it was a fitting place for María to emerge, and to become synonymous with a form of dance that often encapsulated

the bullfight, the battle, the war. In New Mexico, cultural contact was not always peaceful; in addition to the Spanish, conflicts with other Native groups were common. In 1821, a new conduit of influence began when the Santa Fe Trail opened, and traders from the Eastern US began to arrive in increasing numbers. Sixteen-year-old Kit Carson came to Taos with such a group of traders in 1826, and after a long career of exploration and military conquest, made it his home in 1843. His house, now a museum, is still a landmark near Taos Plaza, where the sense of the "Old West" mixes with both the Native and Spanish cultures.

Beginning in the early 1900s, artists began to flock to the US Southwest. Those drawn to Taos established the Taos Art Society in July of 1915. This society was made famous by the Taos Six, a group of famous painters: Joseph Henry Sharp, E. Irving Couse, Oscar E. Berninghaus, W. Herbert Dunton, Ernest Blumenschein, and Bert Phillips. Other artists and writers and personalities

Image of María in 1955 performing ballet on the Taos Plaza, a place more synonymous with Anglo parades in honor of Kit Carson or Hispanic processions in honor of the Virgin Mary or native dances hosted by Taos Pueblo for the tourists to enjoy. By defiantly performing something alien to many viewers in Taos, María fought to break free from the smallness of the town's confines, and to instead ultimately make the world her stage.

such as D.H. Lawrence, Nicolai Fechin, and Joseph Fleck joined an artists' colony that drew a constant stream of visitors and temporary residents.

Taos and the surrounding region also drew women artists, collectors, and patrons, and strong women in particular. Women like Mabel Dodge Luhan, Georgia O'Keeffe, and Agnes

Martin began to populate the remote state and stake their artistic reputations there. Even those who did not move to New Mexico found inspiration inside its borders, such as Willa Cather and her tale of New Mexico history in *Death Comes for the Archbishop*.

This mix of cultures must have seemed extraordinary to María when she moved to New Mexico as a small child. To outsiders, the strange trappings and signposts of the past must have seemed almost medieval, like the mysteries of crystal crosses and secret temples and happenings in the mountains and hidden valleys described in *Enchanted Temples of Taos* by Dora Ortiz Vásquez, who retold mystic stories from her mother and from their Navajo maid Rosario ("Ma Ya Yo"). Relics of the Old World could be encountered in forgotten mountain villages, where a sheepherder might speak with a Castillian lisp, using obsolete dialect from centuries past and a continent away. María's visits to surrounding areas, including a trip underground to a kiva helped her to sense the deep meaning such places hold in the indigenous spiritual world. *Taoseños* were inordinately proud of their fascinating heritage, and the New Mexico history taught in grade school was decidedly more colorful than mainstream

American curricula. Given the fact that her mother was a teacher, María had a strong educational background and a concomitant understanding of the world. She knew that old trade routes led to distinct places far across the globe.

It would have been quite easy for people to assume that Geraldine Harvey and her young daughter had sprung up natural-born in the heady high mountain environs of Taos. But María did not fit in with the Native culture or with the local Hispanic culture. She visited her father in Puerto Rico at 16, but she appeared as a tourist in her own life, seeming out-of-place in a starched gingham dress midst the palm fronds and sands of the island. In northern New Mexico, she did she not fit in with the Anglo artists who had broken free, in many cases, from their privileged upbringing elsewhere, and who had perhaps come West with intention of defining—or even appropriating—Native culture as their as their aesthetic and their oeuvre.

This was a key aspect of María's personality; that it almost came to matter to her more that she could refuse to be defined by her actual birthplace and circumstances of infancy. This refusal to be typecast made it so that she could not be defined as one of a herd. Rather, she had sprung whole cloth from some mythical being, an Athena from the forehead of Zeus, allowing her to occupy a regal position from any outpost she chose. This form of uniqueness mattered a great deal to María. It was a form of fierce determination to overcome the circumstances of her infancy, in which her father was not present and she and her mother had only each

This Girl Is On Her Toes

By JANE LEVY
St. Katharine's Editor

While phrases such as "Changement jete porte de bras" may sound like a foreign language to most they are quite familiar to ballet students at St. Katharine's School.

Maria Diaz, a junior at St. Katharine's, is teaching ballet to fellow students in the high school and also students in the grade school.

Maria, who comes from Taos, New Mexico, conducts eight ballet classes a week along with carrying a full schedule of studies.

Maria first started studying ballet when she was ten years old while attending St. Mary's Academy in Denver. Later she studied at the Denver Ballet Theatre which is a branch of the rine's Maria held classes of her own, in which she taught not only children but also adults. She said she enjoys teaching adults best and children from nine-

American Theatre in New York. There she had two classes a day each an hour and one half long.

Often the Theatre had guest instructors and Maria studied under Igor Schwezoff, Francesca Romanoff and Vincent Morelli who had danced in the movies with Leslie Caron.

During the two summers and one school year she was in Denver she worked in the productions the "King and I" and also "Oklahoma."

In Taos she studied with Jacques Cartier and Louise Oliver. In the summer of 1956 she concentrated on technique at the Ballet School of Arts in San Juan, Puerto Rico.

Before teaching at St. Katharine's Maria held classes of her years-old to her own age group.

Maria is thinking seriously of becoming a ballet teacher but has no desire to perform professionally.

Maria Diaz (extreme right) instructs students, April Clements and Wendy Robinson at the practice bar and | Margie Fields, Margaret B Nancy Cafouras, seated on (Staff photo)

The Taos News
1958

other in order to face the world. When they moved to Taos after a somewhat nomadic tour of remote posts of duty, they were not part of the Pueblo in any formal way, but the outskirts of town provided refuge. In this way, María belonged to everyone and to no one.

While still existing on the fringes, María fought to make dance her ticket out, and in the process, almost by accident, made Spanish art mainstream. Growing up as she did on the sidelines, it was as if she became keenly aware of all of the disparities of life— in economic and race relations, in social justice issues. These hierarchies of life could

be broken down by supremacy in performance, by mastery of an art form that would catapult her out of the strictures of expectations.

But María did not just become an *impresaria* of flamenco. She reimagined the clichéd and fanciful aspects of flamenco archetypes into something personal and original to herself. She struck out against the trite idea that the female foil of the male was a role worthy of any aspiring young dancer. She wanted to bring in a darker, stronger element, perhaps as a way of reconciling the two sides of her heritage. Who did her soul belong to? The Spanish half

or the Native half? Holding on to one could mean dismissal of the other. Instead of signing her soul away, she dismissed both halves and became her own person. She went to Spain to study dance. She learned and spoke Spanish, owned a rosary and various *santos*—beautifully painted images of Spanish saints. But she also ate Pueblo food and learned Pueblo culture, and she owned smudge sticks, traditional herb bundles burned in American cultures for spiritual cleansing.

Somehow María intrinsically knew how to draw on the well of these disparate things, to drink from both philosophies, to merge what she could together, to fashion her

16

could intermix with the conquered, a link between two ancestral chains that were once at war with each other. The Spanish had subjugated the Indigenous people in the 1500s, although the 1680 Pueblo Revolt successfully expelled the Spanish for nearly a generation. Recent scholarship has shown that the Spanish conquest was not a benign colonial "settlement" but wholesale slavery and war, and tensions still persist between Native and Spanish, although cultural reconciliation is now at the forefront of the social justice agenda. María embodied both bloodlines in her DNA. Could either one—the Spanish or the Native—be called the victor in the battle for her soul? How did she reconcile these two warring halves? How much of that war within became part of her dance journey?

The inherent struggle with her own name meant that María's core identity was typecast as a Catholic Mary, followed by the native name "Woesha" and a Spanish surname. María recalls, "Mother called me 'Woesha' which meant 'Happy Girl'...I think that is what fed me at the core; I knew who I was and what I was about."

own belief system. Her coming-of-age-story is truly extraordinary. Instead of a search for femininity and flourish, she sought to build muscle and to strengthen the spine. Instead of a constant struggle with her dual nature, she dismissed the conflict or incorporated it within her dance with the purpose of fighting the status quo, preferring to stand eternally on her own.

María also struggled against roles that society thrusts on women. For example, she is not thought of as an archetypal mother. Although she excelled at everything, "mother" was certainly not an appellation that she craved. Due to performance schedules and touring abroad, her son was often left with María's mother for long stretches of time. Yet ironically, hundreds

of young girls thought of her as their "Flamenco Madre" and they revered her for the huge role that she played in their development as dancers.

Due to the absolute devotion that she showed to teaching her craft for decades in schools, workshops, and other settings, María was, perhaps in spite of herself, a true matriarch — both epitomizing motherly traits while also establishing a culture and tradition that led to the establishment of flamenco education in American dance schools, and thereby contributing to the art form in a global sense.

The conflicts of the past and the present may give a character like María's a sort of stone-fired quality, a process that brings out an underglaze that isn't always visible but is nevertheless present. In that ancestral chain from time immemorial, the rare improbability that the past can live through to today seemed to be embodied in María as a perfect example of the eventuality that a conqueror

Historical tensions are indeed part of the heritage of New Mexico. But the tensions of modern society also affected María deeply. After World War II and the Korean conflict, New Mexico experienced a large number of Native and Hispanic soldiers returning home from those grand and terrible wars. These men had seen the world and experienced the cruel equality of the battlefield, only to have to return to inequality at home. In New Mexico at that time, Natives who lived on federal reservations were not allowed to vote, although they had been granted citizenship in 1924. A man from Isleta Pueblo, Miguel Trujillo, Sr., a Marine sergeant from World War II, came home to fight yet another battle in 1948 when he undertook a legal fight to win the right to vote. This was an early example of the changes that would result from Civil Rights era. María was affected by this growing tide of revolution around her: the American Indian Movement, *La Raza Unida*, women's rights, farmworker protests, Black Power, demonstrations against the Vietnam War, and other initiatives for social change. All these movements had skirmishes in New Mexico, and María lived among and felt the influences of these profound forces at work.

As far as María's dance journey was concerned, she brought together the two warring halves of Native and Spanish, taking to heart the "bad"/"dark" and the "good"/"light" in each culture to create a many-sided soul. María upset the dimensions of symmetry—combining those warring sides through a sort of origami transformation to create a new, anomalous, and unique geometric shape. A one-off. María could infuse and diffuse cultural styles interchangeably. Instead of making angles that were symmetrical around the circle of performance, she drew her own angles, making sure that she was the center, even when the two main dancers were involved, making sure that she was the sun around which all the planets rotated.

This trait of hers was not an ego thing. In Western dance and song, exceptionalism is the norm; there are principle dancers and soloists, a prima or a diva. Conversely, in Native dance, exceptionalism is not a component. The entire group, chanters and dancers and audience, are all equal participants in a grand communal wheel. The center is constantly shifting. Instead of all eyes on the main character, all eyes are on each other or focused downward

María teaching in Miami in the 1980s. Image, (c) Peggo Cromer.

María teaching at San Juan Pueblo (now Ohkay Owingeh). Private collection.

María teaching at Cochita Espinoza School, 1988. (c) Peggo Cromer.

María teaching at La Fonda in Santa Fe. (c) Brian Fishbine.

Class in the 1990s. Courtesy photo, Elsa Kendall.

María with a student. Image © Don J. Usner.

The knife wing figure in jewelry evokes the lines of María's dance movements.

and inward for the participant's own spiritual devotion. Even the drummers often form a huge circle; no one stands out as a "star" facing the audience for solo recognition. María understood this, and she wasn't trying to promote herself as a prima, she was trying to say that her dance was her gift and hers alone. It was her statement to make. She would make her own statement and stand by it, even though flamenco's copyright is in the public's domain.

Something from María's existence in New Mexico imparted an ancient epic story directly into her soul. The state has always been a transit point for beings arriving from far away. Spanish conqueror Don Diego de Vargas wrote in his journal that he had found a land "remote beyond compare." Surviving against great privations in a craggy and lonely and unforgiving space often meant that people were forced to forge strange

alliances and communities. Somehow, that rugged existence inspired others to travel and make their home in desolation. In modern times, even people from wealthy backgrounds decided to chuck it all and move "off the map and off the grid" to New Mexico. What could provoke someone from the comfort of the known to pick up and move to this unknown or forgotten place, traversing great lengths under arduous conditions?

María sensed the draw and pull that the state had on people from elsewhere, and from this admixture of old-timers and newcomers, María could tell fate from destiny. She could discern the difference between being trapped by circumstance and searching for something, so she knew how to create her own journey. New Mexico was, after all, a constant stage for adventurers coming and going. María could distinguish between imitation versus emulation, so even her studies in Spain taught her that she didn't want to be a replica of another artist, no matter how great. She went to Spain to study, but she would not be the progeny of Greco or Amaya, preferring instead to create a passion of her own, just as waves of newcomers to New Mexico had done by reinventing themselves far from their particular point of origin. They emerged in New Mexico re-born, casting off their former lives. María was equally adept at native Sundance as she was at the Bossa Nova, but she aimed to become perfect at flamenco, with her own artistic direction.

This transformation also gave María clues on how to perform.

She knew instinctively that she had to break out of the strictures of expectations. She had to be different, so she was rough and akimbo and contorted and angry. On fire. She couldn't settle for being romantic, traditional, conventional and expected. So even though she knew flamenco conventions perfectly, she celebrated liberation from those staid constraints. It was good to be bad. Being a bit improbable would give her the upper hand to startle the status quo and challenge normalcy. So like lightning in the immense New Mexican landscape or the striking sight of the Pedernal promontory of Georgia O'Keeffe country, she knew that she had to be the largest flower around. Out-sized. Full frame. One to one ratio. And that it was okay to show your bones.

Like any art form, genius practitioners of dance are always building on the past, on those who came before. So much of dance movement is not original. But María endeavored to make sure that her choreography was at least on the edge of something new, like a volcanic ridge forming over the stump of an ancient eruption. By overlaying traditional flamenco form on the indigeneity of being New Mexican, María knew that she could create her artistic reputation on the bedrock of her emergence from a particular place. And that even if it was a barren rock in the desert, she could flower there.

Some Native Americans are reviving a name that some Native cultures used for the northern American continent: Great Turtle Island. A look at a map makes it apparent that the shelled creature, with the fins of Baja California and Florida protruding from the mainland, was a land that experienced an entire history of geological and cultural transformation before new waves of migrants came ashore, and that its outline did indeed bring to mind an amphibious relation. In New Mexico, many a violent upheaval is recorded in nature, and prehistoric evidence is all around, ever-present, and part of modern life. A sense of the past is everywhere in the state: strange rock outcroppings and fossilized bits of eons past dot the landscape like nowhere else on earth. The shift of ancient tectonic plates could make an ocean disappear, leaving meadows full of seashells exposed to high altitude sunshine. This immense past infiltrated María's being and her aesthetic. She intuited her ancient connection to Taos even if she wasn't born there, somehow knowing that what was once there could end up here.

Cherokee author America Meredith says that dance from the plains tribes typically involves "the act of looking, warfare, seeing things from different angles." As the dancer swirls, even if staying in place, the head and arm movements rotate, sometimes in gyroscopic fashion, to new angles. One example of the cultural synchronicity of New Mexico is the fact that the Taos Indians were more connected to Plains Indians than other Pueblos in the state due to their ancestral trade routes, and later, the Santa Fe Trail. Even today, Taos Pueblo's annual Pow-Wow shows the mix of dance and regalia styles.

In contrast, Pueblo dance has deep ceremonial meaning, even if it may appear to be more circumscribed in fluidity of movement compared to

Plains dance forms. As Jemez Pueblo artist Cliff Fragua (who took dance lessons from María) describes it, dance is the ceremony that means that the crops will grow, the rain will fall, the hunt will be successful, the world will keep spinning, and we will be as one with our environment. María's choreography instinctively fused these two forms of tribal dance together. All these elements typified María's use of the floor in flamenco: she would approach, cut away, return from a different angle. Some similarities can be detected in the way a cry and its use in Native dances has parallels to the anguished cry of the *cantaor* in flamenco.

María, one of the nation's foremost figures in the flamenco world, has an origin story as murky as the mantilla that sometimes cloaked her gaze. She was a native of Minnesota, but in reality, it was New Mexico that gave her a place of emergence. When she rose up out of the kiva, visiting as a newcomer, she emerged as someone else, someone truly from New Mexico.

What may appear as anonymity is actually communality.

It was her rebirth. Although perhaps deceptive, the story of her Taos origins was who she truly was, a child of a forlorn place that had a fierce pride in being other, different, unique, irreplaceable, like no other. So it did not matter what the birth certificate said: she was a creature of New Mexico. She swore her allegiance to the Zia flag. When she brought her husband Cecilio from Spain to New Mexico, she was bringing him *home*. By giving birth to her son in the Land of Enchantment, she was finding her corner of the universe. Although María danced for movie stars and for kings and queens, she happily spent decades teaching school kids. This loyalty to New Mexico is a through-thread in every role she ever played. Her core persona as a New Mexican was true to her heart: even though she would never be part of a Catholic parish or a tribal council, she was an archetypal New Mexican.

An image of a Catholic chapel near San Ildefonso Pueblo serves as a visual reminder of the deeply etched overlay of cultures in New Mexico.

New Mexico history is preserved in a way unlike any other American place. The overarching theme of everyday life is the persistence of the past. People live in two-hundred-year-old adobe homes. They worship in centuries-old *kivas* or *moradas*. Streets, foods, topographical features, and everyday articles all bear names from the past: Montezuma Street, *atole*, Sangre de Cristo mountains, *comal* are just a few examples. Advertisers trade on the ways in which this history adds cachet, randomly assigning names such as "Aztec" or "Chaco" to commercial products or designs. María instinctively knew that trading on her faraway unfamiliar looks and her origin would put her in this category of things that had exotic-sounding appeal.

Although New Mexico has often been a battleground for various cultures fighting for dominance, the result cannot be described as one dominant culture totally subsuming others. Santa Fé was the setting for the First American Revolution on what is now present-day American soil, the Pueblo Revolt of 1680. When the Spanish returned, dominance of the Natives was not as severe as before, and the Pueblo system gave an uneasy truce to the discord. Pueblo historian Joe Sando described how both Spanish and Native families suffered from the raiding Comanches, Apaches and Utes, and how the horse and the gun of the Spanish helped defend against these raids. The situation is similar with spiritual practices. After the Pueblo Revolt of 1680, the returning Spanish did not completely obliterate Native spiritual practices as

they had tried to do in the past, so subsequent communities grew up around or using both a *kiva* and a Catholic chapel, celebrating both practices. Different settlements retained their special characters when the region became part of the United States. The Pueblos were sovereign nations scattered throughout the state, and while tribal lands sometimes formed a "checkerboard" pattern adjoining state, federal, Spanish land grant, and other lands, the basic character of discrete areas remained true to its people. With the addition of Anglo settlements, artist colonies, and hippie squatters, New Mexico became a crazy quilt for a unique mix of cultures, not a melting pot as much as perhaps a *cocido*, where flavors blend but each retains its character. The mixture is aided by the fact that the state is etched by trails old and new: The Camino Real,

The Santa Fe Trail, Route 66. This range and variety of special places interconnected by a web of trails means that syncretism informs much of New Mexico's cultural blend. Additionally, this diversity and constant influx of "others" makes for constant change in intercultural relations, often peaceful but sometimes in conflict. Though often in transit or turmoil, the distinct cultural groups pay honor to the past. For example, Taos Pueblo, or Tau-Tah, the place of the Red Willows, is reverting to this ancestral name. Other tribal communities are changing their names back to ancestral names, or deleting the reference to the Spanish "pueblo" in favor of original names.

Much of María's story is sourced in these blurred lines between fact and fiction. She never let the fact that she wasn't born in Taos prevent her from using the place as her point of origin, allowing writers and interviewers to believe what they thought was the truth, and she never bothered to correct articles that came out saying that she was a native New Mexican or a Pueblo woman. Even when modern research tools made it easy to search out birth certificate information and reveal the truth, this biographical detail was left uncorrected. The revision was unnecessary because at that point María had come to completely epitomize Taos. It was almost as if Taos could not be Taos without her as part of its mythology, and María knew that any duplicity was of benefit to the overall scheme of making New Mexico famous.

There is an inexplicable quality that is "Taos." Taos represents the dichotomy between rich and poor, privileged and outsider.

Millionaires jet into town to stay at secluded adobe compounds and dine on European cuisine after skiing the mountains of Taos Ski Valley. Meanwhile, the vendors and hippies and adobe "earthship" builders struggle to eke out a meager existence on the edges of town. The Pueblo of Taos is renowned for its rich traditional culture but is also known for the avant-garde exemplified by artists such as fashion designer Patricia Michaels and musician Robert Mirabal.

Part of the Taos mystique is that the humbler parts of town are as much a draw for the tourists as the rich areas, just as it is in Santa Fé and elsewhere around the state, making all of New Mexico something of a *duende*-draw to others. The fabled "Land of Enchantment" isn't based in wealth or fame but in the fact that you can be yourself in the state and still be accepted. It is the native New Mexican's birthright to be labelled "unique" and "authentic" even when penniless. Further, the claim to being a native of New Mexico is a life-long label, no matter

where New Mexicans end up. The popularity of New Mexican foods such as Hatch green *chile*, *posole*, tamales, and salsa all attest to the enduring influence of New Mexican culture. By affixing its brand to someone not native-born to New Mexico, the ruse of a Taos birthplace aided María's ability to rise out of her circumstances and transcend her origins. And by promoting María as its own, New Mexico received credit for the success of a favorite, albeit adopted, daughter.

Native Americans occupy a stressful dual role. They must traverse between two or more cultures on a daily basis. They must learn and speak Spanish and English, as well as their own mother tongue, and possibly other dialects. Natives participate in village culture and Catholic Feast Days that contain elements of two religions. They may have to observe Anglo rules and customs. These conflicting roles create a constant state of flux.

Martha of Taos, a broomstick skirt emporium.

Pop Chalee means "blue flower" in Tiwa. In the year that Chalee was born, US President Theodore Roosevelt seized most of Taos Pueblo lands including Blue Lake, which was central to the sacred beliefs of the tribe. During María's lifetime, Blue Lake was finally returned. Photos of Pop Chalee by Charles E. Lord. Images courtesy of Tony E. Martinez.

Without the luxury of a cultural status quo, you must constantly be anticipating what is next or analyzing what has just occurred. Dancers are extremely intelligent, and must also be spatial thinkers, translating the geography of choreography to the floorboards and to the other dancers, in one with the music, keeping time, and following the flow. With a dancer's brain, there is a strategy for the chessboard of daily life; watchful against the "other side" and memorizing steps in reverse or backwards while simultaneously counting time. Any particular strategy that can help you in Anglo culture can hurt you in another culture. María's choreography somehow expressed this constant state of being guarded, because her floor work was characterized by a twirl that could double back in pirouette— once with a smile, the second time with a grimace. She knew that she was simultaneously

an outsider, an insider, and not an outsider—a quantum existence that was always dependent on the observer's definition of who she was at that moment.

In New Mexico, the condition of being both outsider and insider has been juxtaposed by the necessity for people to get along. With the influx of various tribes, the warring Spanish, and the land grab of Manifest Destiny, each succeeding group found that the harsh existence in the high desert meant that you had to be able to rely on each other to survive. A scholar from Ohkay Owingeh Pueblo (formerly San Juan Pueblo) Alfonso Ortiz, Ph.D. stated: "Cultures are not automatically antithetical. We can make choices, borrowing what we want from other worlds while keeping our independence."

To answer the question of why New Mexico was the place of María's emergence, we can see that it could only have been in the cosmic landscape of New Mexico that her unique talent could have emerged. New Mexicans are extraordinarily strong and resilient. The privations of the rugged landscape and struggles for power have defined its people. María stood out as a leader, despite being divided internally with genetic makeup from two continents. It seems an absurd improbability that a young woman from here, there and everywhere should land on the international stage, but María used New Mexico as her point of convergence where she could both hold steadfast to her own nature while also becoming fluid between divergent cultures, making the contradictions of her origin and her life into her greatest strengths.

The Río Grande Gorge Bridge, at 656 feet above the river below, is one of the ten highest bridges in the United States. The arch of the bridge seems precariously suspended over the huge canyon cliffs, like a "bridge to nowhere" on top of the Taos mesa. The long drive to Taos through the river bed requires a steep climb, with the traveler's arrival at the mesa top making for a disconcerting encounter with a startling view: paired with the sight of Wheeler Peak, the highest point in New Mexico, often called "Taos Mountain," looming over the area, the distance from mountain top to river bottom has a visual illusion of rending the core of the earth open for display. The mountain stands guard over the town of Taos and Taos Pueblo, one of the longest continually inhabited communities in the country. It is easy to be struck by the fact that this place has a rare confluence of influences and cultures. Something about the particular formation of land and sky has brought so many artists to New Mexico, and to Taos in particular, that the name is now synonymous with creativity and flair.

CHAPTER TWO - A MIGRATION STORY

Flamenco is accompanied by music and song, but also by the percussive sound of hands clapping (*palmas*), fingers snapping (*pitos*) and so on. María often favored *seco*, striking the two hands together in a convex shape that creates a dry clap not unlike an echo in the barren open land of New Mexico where sound ricochets through canyons and outcroppings like a rock skipped from the sky.

María says that she never truly felt like she belonged to the Spanish side of her heritage because she was raised by her Native American mother, and because her Puerto Rican father was absent during significant periods of her life. But Spanish culture did, at least on the surface, gradually come to dominate her public persona because she became an expert at Spanish dance. She was awarded the highest art honor that the country of Spain bestows: *El Real Orden de Isabel la Católica*. María's name became synonymous with Spanish art, and her image was a glittering iconic vision of a Spanish cultural archetype.

The difficulty of not entirely belonging to Spanish culture was compounded by the predicament that María didn't really belong to the Native side of her heritage either. Her mother's Algonquin, Iroquois, Chippewa, Ojibwe and Oneida heritage was far from home. Further, the mother-daughter life was not centered in tribal communities much because of their gypsy sojourn around the western United States, often near Bureau of Indian Affairs schools but far from a place of belonging. When they finally settled in Taos, they lived in the town proper, a community with the northern New Mexico Latin/Hispanic culture, not in Taos Pueblo, the ancient Native settlement. So María was to gain nothing of pueblo culture or tradition except what she garnered by instinct and adaptation. Consequently, right from the beginning, María was a maverick. An imposter of sorts. Bound to no tribe. María adopted Taos because Taos had adopted her. It was an exchange that made the whole barter valid.

María's relation to her Native heritage has connections to the tragic history of traditional cultures that were conquered by the dominant U.S. culture. One particularly sad chapter had to do with tribal children. Until the mid-20th century, the Federal government often placed Native American children in boarding schools, where the intent was to assimilate the children into American ways. María's mother, like many children of her generation, went to boarding school and did not learn her Native tribal languages. Even after the government ended this practice, Native children were

María invades Spain, late 1960s.

often removed from their homes into state child welfare systems or adopted into non-Native families. With the enactment of the Indian Child Welfare Act in 1978, tribal governance requires that tribes raise their own children, so that, for example, adoptions outside the tribe were not typically approved. The purpose is to preserve Native culture as the top priority. Apache artist Bob Haozous refers to the reasoning as having to do with a tribal asset. Children are viewed as belonging to the tribe, and the concept can be extended so that animals and nature are also part of the tribal family. The Native concept of "all our relations" means the love of everyone, everywhere, always.

The Ghost Dance spiritual movement that led to the massacre of over 150 Sioux—nearly half women and children—at Wounded Knee in 1890 is an example of how tensions between traditional and dominant cultures extend to religion and the arts as well. In the US during María's childhood, many Native religious practices were

illegal, and this extended to dance. Imposition of concepts of private property and real estate title often prevented access to sacred lands where religious dance was meant take place, and ceremonial items such as eagle feathers were often restricted. Before the Indian Religious Freedom Act of 1978, this meant that many elements of religion had to be practiced in secret, at peril of arrest and/or imprisonment. Even after legal reforms were made to these prohibitions, law enforcement's compliance with the changes was spotty at best; for example, nuisance, disorderly conduct, and unlawful assembly rules were used to repress Native freedom. This meant that fear was always a routine part of Native life. Only recently have Natives been able to speak freely, if they wish to, about ancient belief systems. Further, with the rise in environmental justice movements, conducting ceremonies publicly has come under newly-revived scrutiny. For example, there have been arrests for conducting ceremonies at Standing Rock and for similar protests to protect national parks and native lands against the ill-effects of extractive industries. Proposed and pending legislation threatens to criminalize protests in ways that will disproportionately impact tribes given their proximity to natural resources, reverence for the water and hunting grounds, and so on.

Simultaneous to arrests of Natives performing religious ceremonies at environmental protest sites, monuments to the past are beginning to topple across the United States, primarily in the southern states where Confederate and colonial icons and structures

halves of her heritage, Native and Spanish, that in most conflicts create a conundrum. The Spanish "side" could no more overpower the Native side than the Native side could resist its conqueror. This irregularity in María's essence made it so that she gained supreme fluidity and malleability with any emotion, culture, or theme. She was equally at home on the grand stages of the world as she was on the earth-packed plazas and pueblos of New Mexico. Although she became a technical practitioner of the Spanish arts in general, and flamenco in particular, her status as a doyenne meant that her unique style transcended the art form. Even under the assumption that her Spanish half had in essence conquered the Native half, so that people assumed that she was mostly Spanish, nothing betrayed her Native half. The Spanish heritage was perfectly embodied in her carriage, her regal bearing, and her use of *lingua español*. In contrast, anyone meeting her and knowing only of her Native heritage would find that nothing betrayed that Spanish self. She carried each culture in her soul, and either could shine when and if

needed. Without any artifice or design, her very existence and ultimate embodiment of flamenco portrayed the warring dichotomy of a flamenco dancer: a refugee born out of fear, a victim of prejudice, fleeing into hiding, forced into the shadows—dancing in caves or by campfires— but always poised to scale the castle walls or flee to the countryside. That mind-set seemed to inform her stance in her art, and it suited her perfectly.

There are many works that María will leave behind. No single magnum opus rises against all the others; rather, her entire life work, seen as a whole, is so imbued with her extraordinary personal story that it has universal appeal, untethered by any tie to country, language, or culture. María is

predominate. Very few new public statues have been erected that replace symbols of oppression with honored leaders of Native America. A notable exception is the Cliff Fragua statue of Po'Pay in Statuary Hall in Washington, DC. Despite the fact that monuments to Native leaders and/or cultures are seldom found in American dominant society, María achieved stature as a cultural icon with a distinct and instantly recognizable look, transcending the constraints that make so many Native leaders faceless to mainstream America.

María has never been forced to resolve the two disparate

PUEBLO

Depósito Legal M. 16 - 1958

Director: Emilio Romero

ROBLES

BARCELONA-13 · CJO. DE CIENTO, 366 · T. 2251393-95-2251963
MADRID-5 · PEÑUELAS, 8 · TELEFONO 239 34 00
MURCIA · CARMEN, 5 (QUITAPELLEJOS) · TELEFONO 17637
VIGO · ECUADOR, 42 · TELEFONO 23401

Año XXV ☆ Número 7.747 ☆ Dos pesetas ☆ Huertas, 73 ☆ Tel. 227-39-91 ☆ Madrid ☆ Martes 28 ☆ Julio de 1964

LOS NEGROS U. S. A. PUEDEN ESTAR ARMADOS

«YO FUI TESTIGO DE LA NOCHE SANGRIENTA DE HARLEM»

PUEBLO comienza hoy la publicación de un apasionante reportaje escrito por un español, testigo excepcional de la violencia desatada en el barrio negro de Nueva York.

«Yo fui testigo de la noche sangrienta de Harlem» es el relato estremecedor de un periodista, corresponsal de Europa Press —José Carlos García Fajardo—, que fué golpeado, magullado y herido mientras buscaba la información que hoy comenzamos a publicar en página 24.

● En el mundo de color, el blanco lleva la iniciativa de crueldad

● La población negra norteamericana representa el diez por ciento de aquella nación

NUEVA YORK, 28. (Crónica de nuestro corresponsal, Manuel Blanco Tobio, por telex.)—De un tiempo a esta parte, algunos americanos controvertibles parecen reservar para la Prensa alemana sus declaraciones más sensacionales. Esto es lo que ha hecho, por dos veces, Goldwater, y lo que acaba de hacer James Baldwin, un escritor negro americano que suele hablar y escribir con elocuencia en nombre de su raza.

Baldwin ha dicho en una entrevista para «Der Spiegel»

Esto de que los negros han estado escondiendo armas lo hemos oído por aquí con alguna frecuencia. No hace mucho leímos en una revista bien informada que en cada casa negra de Mississipi hay escondido, por lo menos, un rifle. En Harlem, cada vez que la Policía practica un registro a fondo, da con un pequeño arsenal.

Las declaraciones de Baldwin fueron ayer mismo confirmadas por la Policía de Nueva York. La Prensa cita a un teniente de la fuerza, afirmando que sólo en la sección Bedford-

... descansa en Benidorm

El máximo goleador de la pasada temporada, Ferenc Puskas, pasa sus vacaciones en Benidorm. Allí descansa y repone fuerzas para cuando llegue el momento de volver a calzar las botas. El artillero madridista tiene que atender a los numerosos admiradores que tiene en la bella ciudad mediterránea. En la foto aparece con uno de sus más jóvenes «hinchas». (Foto Fiel.)

¿Jugará DI STEFANO contra el Madrid en el primer partido de Liga?

Si no le tienden en Italia un puente de oro, es probable que fiche por un año con el Español.

(Página 17.)

FLAMENCO INTERNACIONAL

Una de las chicas se llama María Díaz; la otra, Massuci Okada, y el muchacho es el holandés Jan Drobslach. Los tres forman parte del ballet español de María Rosa, que ayer se presentó en los Festivales de España que se celebran en el Retiro. La pasión flamenca, que Merimé consideraba exclusiva de los gitanos, se ha hecho internacional al abordar las reglas del arte de la coreografía. Los pies de estos artistas excelentes trenzan sobre el tablado el arabesco de la zambra al dictado de una inspiración interior renacida en inesperadas Scremontes. El alma de la copla flamenca encarna en holandés y en japonés sin desvirtuar su sentido, porque todo lo que es verdadero ha de ser por fuerza universal. Así lo entendió el público del Retiro, que tributó al trío flamenco internacional el homenaje de sus ovaciones. (Información, en «Madrid Actualidad».)

Reparte telegramas para pagarse sus estudios

Juan Moreno Monterrubio es un chico madrileño que aprovecha los ratos libres de su trabajo —ocho horas diarias repartiendo telegramas a pie— para estudiar. Espera terminar en septiembre el bachillerato elemental. Pero sus aspiraciones son más elevadas, quiere ser médico. Juan es hijo de un zapatero y tiene diecinueve años. (Información, en Madrid Actualidad. Foto Torremocha.)

El accidente ferroviario de PORTUGAL

CINCUENTA EXCURSIONISTAS SALVARON LA VIDA

● No pudieron subir al tren en Modivas, porque el jefe de estación ordenó que el automotor pasara sin parar.

(Ultima página.)

María is never sentimental, even if the tropes of her chosen dance form often bear clichés as old as time. She does not romanticize her early childhood attraction to dance, saying instead: "It wasn't the kind of thing where I'd gone to see some dance performance when I was a child and said 'Oh, I have to be a dancer.'" She continues, "I was going to a Catholic school, a private school in Denver, and they just happened to have tap dance classes there and this is how it all started. Soon, after we moved to Tucson, I wanted desperately to become a ballet dancer, and there were many ballet teachers there. Then in Taos, ballet teacher Louise Licklider would come up from Santa Fé, and when she stopped coming, there was nothing else to do except try the Spanish dance. I was 15 years old and terribly bored and a friend of mine who also studied ballet taught me a bit of Spanish dance. I soon felt that everything opened up. I liked it very much; I was so very comfortable. Besides, I was beginning to feel uncomfortable with ballet because I was big for my age and I was even heavier than what I am now. I began feeling comfortable with the Spanish dance style because it seemed so much stronger and earthier to me. I think perhaps now that if I had it to do all over again, I would still love Spanish dance, but I sort of wonder in the back of my mind if I wouldn't have gone into modern dance and perhaps relate a bit more to my Indian side. It's just something that is becoming increasingly intriguing to me even though when I got into Spanish dance it wasn't for the purpose of feeling closer to Spain because of my father's heritage but because of my heritage. I still had tremendous doubts as to whether I could do it or not because that is the universal problem for an artist. Are you being true to your heritage? Any artist goes through

more a force of nature, a charge between earth and sky. While she certainly carried the standard as a communal icon, her true genius was more evident in the fact that viewers—her audience—interpreted her impact on a deeply personal level. She was seen as a personal talisman, for use of the vision seeker only. She knew early on that this stance would be her greater legacy—being herself—more than any one performance or piece of choreography. She stood alone in her abilities, and to have seen her perform was a rare and extraordinary privilege, but it was also gone in an instant. Much of the film made of her performances was recorded on poor quality film or video. This defect in the videographic record of her professional life almost doesn't matter, given the impact that seeing her had on so many, and how each person carried away their own personal treasure of memory.

this self-doubt and reflection. And, at that time, the instructors all emphasized that the dancer should have the profound feeling to do Spanish dance—as if you had Spanish blood rampaging through your veins. Anyway, I don't believe in at all that; I think it's a bunch of hooey, but at that time it was a big thing—so much so that at times I had serious doubts as to whether I had necessary fire within me to pull this thing off."

María's deliberate choice not to imbue her past with the trappings of sentiment means that she receives the sole credit for her sheer determination and talent rather than some external force or god-like happenstance that intervened to give her a career. Even though she can be viewed as spiritually half-Catholic and half-Native, she was essentially non-religious in her personal life. New Mexico was and is a spiritual place, with a complex heritage: many practicing Catholics, whose religious traditions often hearken back to practices from colonial times, many Natives with varied and even more ancient traditions, and also a recent history of incomers

whose religions were under the hippie/New Age umbrella. Against this background, María fell through the fissures into her own belief world: belief in art, in hard work, in flamenco. While certainly connected to gypsy and Spanish origins, flamenco swears allegiance to no man. Its followers form a tribe of their own. María did not need to disavow a need for religion as much as she needed to become a novitiate in the great spirit of the individual. The creator, the innovator, the fighter. The sojourner.

Listening to María recount her story is to be swept up on a journey with her out into the world, with the knowledge that the journey would be a transformative one. Leaving the US for Spain as an 18-year-old, she had virtually no help in what can be viewed as an escape from the confines of place and circumstance. In some Native American cosmology and astronomy, everything is written twice; once on the ground and once in the sky. There is a record on earth of astronomical events, even from the faraway past. Similarly, in modern astronomy it

is possible to use our knowledge of the motions of celestial bodies to "go back in time" and verify human records of astronomical events such as comets. In like manner, María seemed to know that she could take an art form associated with the past and make it new and modern. She felt the pull of a timeless rhythm and she yielded to that force to discover a capacity greater than had been previously imagined.

PHOTO GALLERY

RUVEN AFANADOR
KEN HOWARD
BEVERLY GILE
WINTER PRATHER
JACK MITCHELL
BRIAN FISHBINE

RUVEN AFANADOR

KEN HOWARD

BEVERLY GILE

WINTER PRATHER

JACK MITCHELL

BRIAN FISHBINE

CHAPTER THREE - REACHING FULL FLOWER

To dream of a fan relates to affairs of the heart. To fan yourself predicts an embarrassing entanglement; to see others fanning is a warning that you are playing too wide a field; to lose a fan is a sure sign that you're in danger of losing true love through fickle behavior—cool it!
—The Dreamer's Dictionary

The physicality of flamenco is catalogued in a textbook set of movements and expressions: minute curls of the fingers, the downcast gaze, the fiery sparks erupting between the principal dancers, the incessant tapping seemingly aimed at breaking the floor into splinters. Above all, there is that certain look that a flamenco dancer has: a peculiar gaze that is subject to interpretation. Between the male and the female dancers, the woman might be an object of desire. She might be an object of disdain or rivalry. All of these emotions might be real or feigned. The flash of insight from the eyes is vital to the interpretation of the dance story. María says that you must have the ability to transmit the power of what you are saying from your heart. Form is important, but the fire must burn inside of you.

In María's case, she was able to hone her artistic statement by emitting a brilliant fire from her eyes. She could cast her gaze in such a way that it could seem to land into some middle-distance between herself and the intended target: that verge between life and death where those watching might be struck by the feeling that they might die if they did not reciprocate the passionate love she was conveying. Even in repose, perhaps while her dance partner took a turn around the symbolic fire center stage, María still crackled with emotion, she wanted to skirt the fire. She has attributed this ability of hers to the fact that she is "earthy and gutsy," "mean and angry, full of strength and power." She stresses these traits over the trait of "coquettishness" so often identified with the art form. Her mastery of flamenco is so profound that even if she was as still as a statue, María could evoke a dream with the eyes wide open. Or she could close her eyes and call forth a dream-like state that brought the audience along on a trip into the imaginary.

In María's flamenco *ouvre*, there were only two types of dreams: the frantic horror of impending doom, or the swoon of emotion where the dancer succumbs to the joy of romance in a fanciful dream-state that blurs the borders of reality or diffuses the difference between night and day. In either case, María was the ultimate conjurer, making viewers step into the dream before their eyes, turning the performance into a communal experience.

The musical term "decrescendo" means decreasing the volume in a musical composition; the opposite of crescendo. This is not just a mechanical matter of adjusting a knob. The technique of raising or lowering the volume is meant to carry emotional impact. With every build-up, there must be a step down. If the listener must physically lean forward to capture the essence of sound, they become invested in the message. This concept holds true for flamenco. The role of the narrator or lead singer informs the story and sets the stage. After the initial opening song, guitar music and dancers are layered in gradually or with a bolt of light when the performance opens. In a stock version of a flamenco composition, there is a build-up in the intensity as the passion levels rise, followed by the inevitable descent. The dancers appear to search the stage floor for answers to the great questions of life. Silence follows the eruption of passion. It is an art form tailor-made to be incorporated into opera.

Bizet's opera *Carmen,* set in 1830, deals with the love and jealousy of Don José, who is lured away from his duty as a soldier and his beloved Micaëla by the gypsy factory girl Carmen, who eventually leaves him for a bullfighter. In the 1981 Franco Zeffirelli production of *Carmen* for the Metropolitan Opera, the production did not emphasize a dance component. Today, dance is an extremely important part of the opera. Few people may be aware that in 1987, María helped to advocate for the use of more dance, and the hiring of more American dancers on opera stages. Zeffirelli originally planned to bring major dancers from Spain, but when María asked him to consider hiring dancers stateside, and he agreed. A new production of *Carmen* by Zeffirelli followed in 1996, and a new *La Traviata* of his, with María's choreography, followed in 1998. For her own contribution to *Carmen,* María did not play the title role (a role only an opera singer could fill), but her choreography helped to underscore Bizet's theme that "love is a rebellious bird that none can tame." María's design for the dancers in Carmen's troupe encapsulated her own embodiment of the classic hot-tempered and cold-hearted woman, accompanied by a girl gang of cohorts, into the textbooks.

direct. After initial ballet and Spanish dance training in the United States, she traveled to Spain to study and to perform. Key training took place at the school *Amor de Dios* under instructor Victor Eugenia, and she took classes with other leading instructors of the day. She joined the María Rosa Spanish Dance Company, ultimately performing throughout every province in Spain, bringing her singular interpretations of Spanish dance to the mother country in what could be analyzed as a kind of reverse colonization. She also performed in North Africa, Portugal, and South America with large national Spanish dance companies such as the Paquita Rico Company and smaller flamenco groups. After her initial studies and touring in

Spain in the 1960s, she quickly achieved international renown as a performer, choreographer, and director, ultimately achieving the status as one of the finest flamenco dancers of her generation. *The New York Times* praised "the extraordinary force of her technique" with its "distinctive, sinuous style that suits her elongated arched back and expressive arms." Exhibiting a flexibility and innovation found in all great artists, she has been described by critics as "the Baryshnikov of Spanish dance," "brilliant," and "explosive."

With her return to the US, María was doing more than moving across time zones. Somehow she transported the dark shroud of flamenco's past to the sunny American Southwest. Having met her husband Cecilio Benítez in Madrid in 1966, they quickly married, and moved to Taos, where their son Francisco was born in 1967. In 1969, the family moved to Sedona, Arizona where both parents taught at the Verde Valley School for four years. In 1973 the family was back in New Mexico, where María and Cecilio co-founded the *María Benítez*

As with opera, the themes of love, loss, and pain are parts of the tapestry of flamenco. These emotions are never taken for granted or trivialized. They happen to us all. No one escapes them. Despite the universality of these feelings, the only way to convey them is to make it seem as if they have never happened to anyone before. That is what made María's capture of these emotions seem so authentic— as to appear true. The only truth, the one true love. María's *duende* was right before you, and she forced you to not only drink from the same cup, but to drink it to the dregs. Except in María's case, after she had drunk her fill, she threw the cup to the stage and smashed it into bits, metaphorically speaking.

María's route to fame could be seen as circuitous or as very

Teatro Flamenco. The company had a reputation for excellence, with a history of performances at festivals and major concert halls in 49 states and abroad, at over 1600 venues reaching an estimated 7 million people. Over the years, "*Teatro Flamenco*" and "*Estampa Flamenco*," a second troupe of youthful dancers formed in 1991, kept up a blistering pace of performances. For example, between June 1993 and April 1994, performances and residency activities included the following: the State University of New York, Oswego (concurrent with the national conference "Latin America: Diversity in Dreams"); then performances in Dayton, Ohio and Schaumburg,

Illinois; then three performances of *El Amor Brujo* with the San Antonio Symphony; then in Hamilton, Bermuda. The year 1994 also saw performances at the Concert Association of Greater Miami and a California tour including Pepperdine University, UC Davis, California Polytech State University, and Humboldt State University. Later in 1994, it was on to Colorado for *El Amor Brujo* with the Colorado Springs Symphony. Other foreign destinations over the years included Austria, Holland, and Canada.

María regularly performed and choreographed for opera, including an illustrious tenure

at The Santa Fe Opera. Famous for her choreography of the operas *La Traviata* and *Carmen*, she is also widely-known for her staging and performance of *La Vida Breve* and *El Amor Brujo* for the Dallas Opera, premiering in January 1993. Giancarlo del Monaco's production of *La Forza del Destino* at the Met in 1989 was also one of her notable achievements in choreography.

María believes that one of her primary achievements was in *El Amor Brujo*—in which her choreography and performance in Manuel de Falla's dance drama received critical attention after it was televised nationally. It was remounted in San Antonio and Colorado Springs in 1994. Her choreography for *Carmen* for New York Metropolitan Opera was televised nationally in 1997 on PBS Great Performances, and she repeated that performance at the Met in 1998. Another performance from Jackson, MI was also televised on PBS. She also choreographed and staged operas for the Boston Lyric, and for companies in Virginia, St. Louis, Santa Fe, Fort Worth, and Austin. María worked for or performed at the Orchestra of Santa Fe, the New Mexico Symphony Orchestra, and the Milwaukee Symphony Orchestra. The companies associated with her also toured internationally and performed for network and public television, and some performances live on in the cyberverse, such as María's *solea* performance at Jacob's Pillow in 1996, Boston Pops, New Mexico KNME (PBS) shows *¡Colores!*, and "Artisode." María's troupe of "Flamenco's Next Generation" ("Next Gen") dancers appeared with Charles Osgood on the CBS program *Sunday Morning* in 2014. Her appearance on *Perry Como's Christmas in New Mexico*

summer season held for over four decades in Santa Fé, her impact is clear.

Teatro Flamenco was a huge part of the Santa Fé social and cultural scene for many years. Those who knew her would return again and again to her performances; a few examples are New Mexican luminaries such as The Santa Fe Opera founder John O. Crosby, actress Greer Garson, and Nancy Zeckendorf, philanthropist and former ballet dancer. She danced for visiting celebrities such as Princess Grace, Anne Baxter, and Jacques d' Amboise, as well as actors and producers such as Larry Hagman, David Ellis, Merrill Brockway, Anthony Quinn, and Bert Schneider. María interconnected with everyone in a deep way; everything from learning bookkeeping tips from Crosby to sharing workout advice with Tazbah Gaussoin. Her appeal was widespread. Waitresses and plumbers came to see her or to take dance lessons and many wrote fan letters, poetry, or personal notes which speak to her impact on those of all walks of life. At one point, it seemed as if every photographer in town counted an image of her in their collections and artists began to populate posters, postcards, and paintings with her image.

(1979) gave her exposure to a wider American audience, but she reveled in the obscure and the difficult. For example, in 2013 she portrayed the only woman in New Mexico arrested by the Inquisition accused of secretly being Jewish, the imprisoned *Doña Teresa Aguilera y Roche and Intrigue in the Palace of the Governors*, in a "Moments in Time" piece on NMPBS, made for the New Mexico History Museum. In addition to all of her special appearances, the record for her regular gigs— for example, eight seasons at Joyce Theater in New York City, performances at the Kennedy Center and her standing 12 week

By 1983, María and her husband had married the activities of their touring companies to a broader artistic mission. They co-founded the *María Benítez Institute for Spanish Arts* (also known as the "Instituto del Arte Español") as a non-profit educational and cultural organization to preserve and promote the rich artistic heritage of Spain. The Institute used a multi-disciplinary approach that employed art,

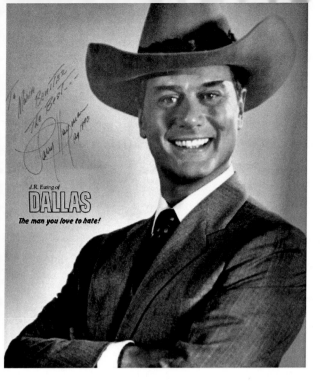

J.R. Ewing of
DALLAS
The man you love to hate!

María's professional endeavors were all about creating opportunities for New Mexicans, or for foreign artists touring abroad. She made inroads helping students in New Mexico's Española Valley, working with leaders such as Roger Montoya. The Institute sponsored master classes, poetry gatherings, and music concerts by internationally known artists such as José Greco, Joaquín Ruiz (Airies de Silencio), the gypsy guitarist Sabicas, Rosita Segovia, Antonio Portanet, Ciro (El Muro), Mario Maya, Roberto Lorca, Manolo Rivera, Victorio Korjhan, Orlando Romero, Javier LaTorre, José Molina, La Tania, Domingo Ortega, Adela Clara, Luis and Juan Ortega, Ángel Muñoz, Antonio Granjero, Rafaela

Carrasco, Eduardo Montero, and Alejandro Granados. The Institute presented exhibitions featuring several photographers, including Candace Bevier and Alicias Maresmafois, and also painters Jesus Aguilar and Francisco Benítez. María and her colleagues performed lecture-demonstrations at elementary schools in Hispanic and Native communities of northern New Mexico. This function was close to María's heart, and she may have been unaware of what it must have been like for a young child to see world class dance performed on the glossy floorboards of a junior high gymnasium. As her classes grew, it was easy to see how the art form of flamenco was taking root in the harsh high desert, and her choreography style began to populate the work of her students as they became professionals.

In addition to working with well-known dancers, she helped to establish or further the careers of those who worked

music, poetry, and theatre to engage all students. The co-founders worked extensively throughout many public and private school systems in and around Santa Fé for many decades. Summer workshops for adults brought in people from around the world, learning guitar, Spanish dance, *Jota* dance, *cante* and percussion (*cajon*).

with her, including Antonio Granjero, Estafania Ramirez, Vicente Griego, Juan Siddi, Ricardo Anglada, and José Valle Fajardo "Chuscales." Chuscales is a flamenco guitarist from Antequera, Andalucía whose formative years were literally spent in the gypsy caves of the region. María also helped women reach their artistic goals. For example, her protégé Emmy Grimm, "La Emi," debuted her inaugural season at the María Benítez Cabaret Theatre in Santa Fé—the same place where she had performed countless times as one of María's "Next Gen" troupe members.

Many of those whom María encouraged have gone on to notable careers. Some have begun companies of their own, such as Antonio Granjero and Estefania Ramirez with "Entreflamenco"; La Emi with "Emiarte Flamenco"; Juan Siddi, with "Flamenco Santa Fe," and Mina Fajardo, in various productions with her husband José Valle Fajardo "Chuscales." In 2019, La Emi was chosen to choreograph and perform in Opera Louisiana's production of Carmen, and the official State of New Mexico Christmas ornament was designed with her image. In these echoes of María's career, the Institute's work to establish or further the careers of others is profound, and will have lasting impact.

The Institute received support from government, corporate, and philanthropic organizations such as the National Endowment for the Arts, the City of Santa Fe, the New Mexico Arts Division, the New York State Council on the Arts, the Lila Wallace-Reader's Digest Fund, the National Dance Repertory Enrichment program, the Mary Flagler Cary Charitable Trust, the Harkness Foundation for the Arts, the McCune Foundation, and the Thaw Foundation. Other support came from the New Mexico State Department of Health (programs to combat childhood obesity) and the Spanish Colonial Society and Museum. For many years, María's students were a staple of the Spanish Market bandstand performances on the Santa Fé Plaza.

Chief among her many accolades and honors, María received the *El Real Orden de Isabel la Católica* in 2006, which was conferred on behalf of Spain's King Juan Carlos by Spanish Consulate General Julio Montesinos. The award, named for Queen Isabella of Castille, is Spain's highest artistic honor. She received both the New Mexico Governor's Award for Excellence in Art and the Santa Fe Living Treasure award. She received the Classical Spanish Dance Award from the Institute of Puerto Rico in New York City, and the golden key to the city of Miami. She was named a Notable New Mexican by the Albuquerque Museum in 2009. She has served on many arts panels, including those of the National Endowment for the

Arts and the City of Santa Fe Arts Commission. When Cecilio passed away in January of 2014 in NYC at age 80, María's own career began to draw to a close.

This snapshot of her formal career shows how intensely María devoted herself to the task of spreading the flamenco gospel. The paramount "through line" in María's life was authenticity. She

Although much of María's fame was pegged to her individuality as a solo performer, she was also known for famous partnerships, such as with the incomparable Vicente Romero.

could not tolerate the superficial, the cosmetic, the popular. She could juxtapose the African beat against a costume with an Elizabethan cuff, or send an elbow akimbo to cut through a dainty line. She might wear pants to dance freely, or a backless dress to show every muscle in her frame. The stock image of a flamenco dancer swathed in a sea of polka-dots, captured by petticoats, and tortured by tight heels, trapped in a spiraling death-on-stage was something that María hated. She challenged the confines of the aesthetic that restricted women to their

stereotypical roles. In flamenco, no matter how shabby the floorboards or broken the *cajón*, the performance could create an entire life story of star-crossed lovers or the end of a epoch. Sometimes, María's role would shift imperceptibly so that she could ignore traditional culture or gender roles. She knew the hardship of persecuted peoples, both Native and Spanish, and her early visits to Spain instructed her on the age-old persecution of the gypsy people. Especially in the aftermath of World War II, there was a European sensibility that the air contained the ashes of the

dead, the persecuted Jews and gypsies. So the metaphor of fire was electric in its implications: we dance around campfire, but the air it exhales contains the ashes of the dead. We are literally and figuratively close to tragedy. To the heart of the pain. María took these deeper issues to the fore.

In María's performances, this awareness of persecuted peoples and the complex role of the woman forced the typical dueling roles of flamenco into sharp relief. Men, of course, are half of the romantic equation necessary for the flamenco calculus, but one of María's great innovations was that she defied tradition. Even with a partner, she essentially stood alone on stage, commanding obedience. Even if flamenco owes much of its culture to torrid romance and unrequited love, María's performances also defied those notions because she didn't believe in those things. She was in many respects a woman from a traditional culture, who married for love and upheld conventional values, but there was no way that she would let her career stand for soap opera emotions or trite romance. Her stoic grief was real, not feigned.

María's story is more than a demonstration that she was a product of her times. She brought about change of her own, within the greater context of changes in the art world that emerged with the civil rights movement and the women's movement. Women of color broke barriers. Gender politics yielded to the sway of changing norms. And María

was a woman at the forefront of these changes. She was a businesswoman. She had musical talent. She knew light and paint and staging. She knew how to be tough or how to use her feminine wiles, as circumstances dictated, but always to pursue her goal, not in vindication of someone else's point or power play but in the service of her own art.

In the many decades traversing the globe, María never lost who she was at heart: a woman from an innocent time and place, who despite the whirlwind cosmopolitan scenery of international fame, always wanted to look back at beloved New Mexican vistas of mountains and cactus and waves of blue gramma grass.

To watch the black-hawks circle their prey. To hear the ancient beat of Pueblo drums. María's dignity translated to a special kind of power, a presence conversant with both royalty and the everyday people, allegiant to no one culture, yet enthralled by all of them. That specialness kept her apart from any group, on the fringes of society, not unlike the

fringe of her elaborate shawl, with her audience watching as it fell in a solitary spiral with a move that began above her head and followed in a cascade down to her feet. She owned the control of that spiral. She held that power and understood its essence. She captured the essence of its ballet, defied time as if to stop it in free fall—as if to say, "watch this: you will never see it again."

Defining María's femininity is difficult. She certainly knew exactly how to control reactions to her beauty; she knew how an almost electrical sense of beauty and desire can be communicated in a performance. In traditional cultures, lightning is often described as sent by the gods, whether as a punishment or as a sign of a transforming rain to come. Western scientific explanation describes a more complicated relation between earth and the heavens. Cloud-to-ground lightning sends an invisible path of negatively

charged electricity from the sky to the ground, where objects are usually positively charged. From the ground, a path of positive electricity flows almost instantaneously upwards, to meet the negative charge and create the flash of lightning that we see. Mythology in many cultures gives us thunder gods such as Thor, Zeus, Perun, or Indra, but female symbols of the earth can also carry a spark of electricity. María was at once masculine in her wielding of the electric power that she possessed and feminine in her adherence to societal and dance conventions about how the female dancer is supposed to look and to act.

María's performances often conveyed a paradoxical approach to the tension between the masculine and the feminine. She detested having the woman cast as the romantic rescue or the helpless ingenue or the hapless victim of Cupid's arrows ... unless the guise of helplessness could be used as part of a scheme to reveal the truth, or to expose the cad for who he was. This double-cross was there—if you knew to look for it—and was described by one viewer as feeling "gypped by a gypsy." She detested being the object of romantic ardor in the classic flamenco set piece. She had to fight off advances in the real world and developed her awareness of the feminine role even before the women's movement, so it was an act of subversion to slyly incorporate this defiance into her choreography. There is that moment in the dance—that flirtation and resistance of the classic love story— when the dancer whips back, first turning away as if to second-guess or

María wanted to be known for her muscle and spine, and that is why photos of her back are so telling of her inner person.

contemplate the next move, and then instantly turning back toward the partner. This moment can be construed as the moment of self-discovery when the woman cleaves to the man—they are, after all, to become one, and she is to sublimate her self into his superior being. María,

however changed this movement into a self-actualization in which she was turning back to her own self. Rather than being an actress charged with embodying the laws of attraction, she focused on the paradoxical response—the act of repelling. In this way she never became an object of the male. She was an object unto her self. While the male half of the dance might lay claim to the title of lightning rod, María found her own way to strike and destroy. You might see his flash on stage, but she was the unseen charge reporting back to the heavens. Or she was perhaps something other than a path for electrical charge; more of a sacrificial point designed to collect the charge and divert the danger away from an intended object. If her electric charge

An apocryphal story posits that a different boot was placed each week on María's dressing table in vain attempts to vie for her affection.

was escape or protection, like a lightning rod, it was her way of saying that while the male may have thrown the bolt, she caught it and diffused it. She was thus fighting societal convention with strength, matching the male dancer.

In flamenco, the shawl or *mantón* carried by a female dancer makes her into a veiled being, by definition mysterious and aloof. But mystery is beyond good or evil because its true nature is not revealed. Until it is revealed, the essential quality exists in a quantum state of neither and both. Romantic betrayal and heartbreak are some of the many themes of flamenco, and those afflictions can change the dancer into good or evil, depending on the outcome and how she reacts to it. To a young María discovering both Spanish dance and her own being, these had to be very sophisticated topics. The Spanish Catholic response to sexuality was extremely conservative, as are the cultural mores of Native tribes. Sexual restlessness as a thrilling and dark concept may either come from a place of personal experience or from the requirements of the "role" assumed by the actress inside the dancer. While the dancer's inner world might be roiling with passion, the surface could appear quiet and unbroken, or the opposite could be true if the main dancers were actually in love. María did not have any qualms about betraying her stage lover, night after night betray him on stage, or hiding her true feelings if need be because once she entered the flamenco realm, she left both the Catholic and the tribal worlds far behind.

María epitomized the archetypal powerful woman. She employed animal persuasion to get her way. She would literally show her teeth, lower her head, and glare. The effect was startling to those who didn't know that it was an act. Animal persuasion came with an animal percussion. Everything staccato. The clacking of the castanet. Sharpness in heel and in elbow and in the flick of wrist. The clap was *seco* (dry and hard). María's hairdo was utterly tight, with every hair pulled back and formed into a tight knot, and fire erupted from her eyes. The fan snapped open and closed. Her shawl flung out into space in a perfect galaxy of light. Heel and toe and tap in a growing crescendo. María's dance and choreography had an agile energy that was capable of forward and reverse gears at the same time. She could stare at a spot ahead, then snap back with disdain toward her partner or the audience. That forward momentum propelled the viewer into the storyline, providing a visceral understanding, even if the story arc was inaccessible because of a foreign language or lyrics that could not be understood. The device of song paired with dance must have been used in the deep past to convey stories across boundaries and over mountains and

across generations. Sometimes existence was dependent upon the transmission of the story. It was vital to survival.

The flamenco story is a complex exposition. The interplay between the *cantaor* and the dancers makes for constant scene-cutting. To be successful, neither part of this balance can wrest the entire story away from the other. The singer must yield the floor at times to the dancers, becoming more of a commentator or chorus member. Likewise, at times the dancers must be absent altogether, or in stasis. The dancers must also shape-shift to keep up with the story line. In her work, María often had to handle the role of director, even as she danced. JoAnn Garcia Orellana speaks of the times that she witnessed María commanding a hapless

tourist or helpful audience member to stop clapping in time to the proceedings. Her directorial scope was wide and fierce. María could alternate the urgency with which she transmitted the story. She could be emotionally soft or hard, from virginal innocence to an intensity that made for interludes of almost sexual release. But the viewer never had the sense that this intensity was somehow prurient; instead, María was dragging you into the secret lair of the artist to glimpse what the composer or singer was feeling and how her interpretation of their artistry added a layer that created a simultaneity among them all. Despite the obvious separation between dancer and *cantaor* and musical accompaniment, they could become one whole, trembling in intensity.

María could give off the air that she had been startled by a few notes of music—a self-awareness that jazz musicians also seem to possess, that they are physically affected by the music. Watching her, it seemed that she had to absorb, physically, what the music was doing to her, even in the presence of her partner onstage. Or perhaps she was reminding us the earth moves, not the sun. But then she could just as easily sweep that all away, and instead rotate around her dance partner in a way that made it seem again that he was the center of the galaxy. Another time she might seem hell-bent on her partner's destruction as her suitor. She could slyly recast him from romantic foil into a rival, an enemy, or a demon. It felt like she was trying to say that life is hard and painful, love is tragic and forlorn, but you can always fight. This weary weight of the tragic juxtaposed with an evanescent quality made her choreography powerful. After a performance, an audience member could be as physically drained as the performers, and left with a feeling that some cherished thing had been swept away. María's motive and adherence to truth was so painful that it might cause you to look away. This stance should never be mistaken for arrogance or elitism, even if on the surface it could appear that way. Instead, María was suggesting motives that lie deeper in the subconscious. Truth is the devil, and it was a devil that she knew.

In Native cosmology, the ground and the sky both carry the story of the universe. María was similarly living her own truth in a bold and plain fashion, making the dance floor speak. Her body could be understood as sort of a medium between the

cosmic themes of the universe and the plain truth of the dirt, much like lightning striking the ground or a storm producing rain in the dust. Her choreography struck a chord of universal truth in such a profound way that it was almost something to be ashamed of—you saw something that you should not have seen, a flash of intimacy or sexuality or rage. And you felt it too. Her performance left a mark that was permanent in its effect. This ability to convey the primacy of raw and real emotion is a skill that few possess, but María made it her own. It was almost as if she was engaged in a form of thought instead of a physical act of dance. And the thought led to a conclusion: she could strike out against something, or she could turn the energy inward in such a way that the audience might not be sure if they were experiencing the sting of rejection or the swoon of love. She didn't want to portray the angelic virgin or the devil, she wanted to embody a pure

force of energy, capturing angles and movements that, while fleeting, stayed in your emotional memory forever, seared as if by fire. In this way, when it seemed like she was doing something completely novel or avant-garde, those moments also pulled at some ancient memory deep inside her audience. An anvil dance that was the language of the earth. A heartbeat. A drum. A storm strike.

María brought these unique powers to her performance, but also into her actions in the world. As the Civil Rights era of the 1960s and 70s began to change lives in our homes, workplaces, and organizations, María was also beginning to have influence in the arena of art hierarchies. Her actions in both realms hint at what may have been María's core belief system: that a woman was a power in her own right. That she did not need a man. And that she could empower other women.

CHAPTER FOUR - *¡LEVANTATE MUJER!* / DANCE AS ACTIVISM

Certain words do not survive translation; for example, the Spanish word *"flamenco"* technically means "Flemish" and for reasons unknown only later took on an association with gypsies. For whatever reason, the autonomy of the gypsy traveling the world as part of an invisible web is reminiscent of the autonomy of tribal nations in the American Southwest. While sovereign in their own right, these tribes are oppressed nonetheless, and it is under the banner of the quest for freedom that María marched.

The advantage of time shows that as María's professional career took off, the fire of her success was stoked by the flames of social change in the civil rights era. In New Mexico, the land grant movement burst onto the national scene in 1967, when activist Reies López Tijerina and his followers in the *Alianza Federal de Mercedes* took over the Tierra Amarilla courthouse in northern New Mexico. The conflict was based on the loss of lands that had been granted by Spain to families in the region centuries before, a loss that highlighted the importance of local Hispanic heritage. New Mexico, with its proximity to California and Mexico, also felt ripples of the farm workers movement led by Dolores Huerta and César Chávez in the 1960s and 1970s. Other cultural changes came to the region in this period as well. The 1969 movie *Easy Rider*, filmed partially in New Mexico, highlighted the hippie movement with its commune lifestyle. One of the producers, Bert Schneider, came to several of María's performances. Many of the early New Mexico communes were situated in Taos where María had spent a considerable part of her youth. The women's rights movement of the 1970s, as it played out in the art world in New Mexico, had echoes of an older generation of powerful women in the arts, women like Georgia O'Keeffe, Mabel Dodge Luhan, Agnes Martin, Laura Gilpin and many others who changed the economic realities of commerce in art.

It was not that María was seeking to lead a movement. A cause was thrust upon her because she was emblematic of the particular struggle facing Latina and Native dancers. With her rapid success, she was an inspirational symbol for the large minority population of New Mexico and beyond. The New Mexican struggle for identity meant that minority people felt like second-class dwellers on the outskirts of society, unable to break into mainstream or world stages, and by accomplishing this for herself, María served as an example for others. Perhaps her deep consciousness of Spanish conquest and migration were communal memories, somehow implanted by the dance. María was not unaware of this phenomenon and how her presence and ability could make a difference. She recognized that her success and her story meant more than just twirls across a stage. Dance is a form of protest, and the emotional underpinnings of the cause inform the story told on stage. In some ways, María was like a mirror for New Mexico, refusing to be reflected back as a dismissed minority but rather a person to be marveled at, a unique presence able to transcend the confines of expectations. When she did succeed, it changed the world's view of New Mexico and also how a woman of color could rise to the top.

The trouble in María's mind was that she did not want to be defined as a "woman," as if that qualifier before "artist" somehow diminished

her. Her feeling was similar to that of ballerina Maria Tallchief, who emerged from Osage Indian territory to prominence in the ballet world, and was ultimately recognized as America's first prima ballerina. Tallchief said, "Above all, I wanted to be appreciated as a prima ballerina who happened to be Native American, never as someone who was an American Indian ballerina." María had similar misgivings. She did not want special treatment. She did not want to be known as a "female" or a "Native" or a "Spanish" dancer. She also had to struggle against the sexism of the dance world and the opera world and the music world. She could dance as if she was the object of a man's lustful search for sexual satisfaction without actually consenting to being seen in such a way. She invited it but fought it off. Perhaps through the trick of some sort of otherworldly demeanor, she never gave the sense that she was the object or the victim or the ingenue. She was simply The Star.

In the flamenco world, women were striking out for their own voice. Spain's famous Carmen Amaya wore pants in a flamenco performance, at first causing some shock in public reaction. Nancy Zeckendorf, philanthropist and former ballerina, recounts how there was a time when dance was looked down upon as a career goal for young women. When she announced to her parents that she wanted to become a ballerina, they were alarmed and insisted that she see a priest. His advice was that Zeckendorf should resist the aspiration to dance because "all dancers are gypsies who sleep around." María was aware of the rigid societal expectations for women, and she wanted to keep her own composure even as sexual mores and women's roles were changing all around her. She insisted on controlling the exact image that she wanted to project, even if the piece that she was performing had its own particular image. She wanted that image to read "María" even if she was playing the role of someone else.

Part of the hippie movement called on its followers to become more in touch with their emotions and with their connections to nature and to the earth. Art, fashion, dance, and music all followed suit with an explosion of psychedelic styles that evoked the freewheeling communal vibe that spawned Woodstock as well as the Vietnam protests. In this tumultuous mix of styles, flamenco could be viewed as an esoteric niche of ethnic expression slapped with a label of "gypsy" culture, a view that rankled María to no end. Hippie culture could easily co-opt other cultural art as its own, but María would never attest to any association with the hippie movement, even though this movement found refuge in New Mexico's wide-open spaces and multicultural society. Although María credits social justice changes

as helping her career, she preferred to see her art form as successful because it was hard and elemental and precise, not because it was soft or "counter-cultural." New Mexico in this era was troubled by disputes over property, the fight of the Native peoples to reclaim what was seen as stolen land and the protests of land grant activists over the loss of land to the Anglos. The cascade of claims over contested spaces sometimes made New Mexico seem like a battleground of divisions between cultures, much as the Roma had been dispossessed of their homeland and cast out into an unwelcoming world. But the counterculture belief that all property was shared or communal did not appeal to María, despite the fact that flamenco was sourced from a huge pool of shared experience. María did believe in property rights, in intellectual rights to one's art and the value of artistic contributions. María put her stamp on what belonged to her.

María's success was certainly helped by the civil rights era that benefitted women, Hispanics, and Native American people. National explorations of cultural identity contributed to María's ability to sell her work as inherently authentic, springing as it did from a state whose heritage lent itself to a growing cultural awareness. She intuited that the art that she was promoting was part of a larger movement to promote Hispanic heritage and culture and that no other place except New Mexico demonstrated so perfectly this nexus between art and social and cultural causes.

María's complex role as a wife and mother was unfolding simultaneously to the women's movement. She was a working mother, who worked closely with her husband, but with her success pinned to long hours on the road touring, her son was often left in the care of María's mother. The Native and Latina roles of traditional motherhood with attendant cultural associations were sometimes at

"Passion and dignity"
—The New York Times

"One of the finest exponents of Spanish dance today"
—Boston Herald

"She took the audience by storm"
—Dance Magazine

"A crackling display of temperament and discipline"
—The New York Times

"Undoubtedly one of the greatest dancers today"
—Denver Post

odds with roles in society at large. María had to grapple with how her role as a mother could change depending on where she was and who she was with, but her abilities in handling shifting roles made her adept at the process. She stayed true to her core self. María certainly moved in mysterious ways, living through herself, not living through others, not conforming to societal strictures about motherhood and so on. She has ascribed her philosophy on these issues to the fact that she always felt that she was created as an artist first, as a mother second, and that she had no choice but to follow her prime directive as if it were her faith.

This mindset must have contributed to María's great success. Her own brand of flamenco rose to the fore, and it affected her audiences so profoundly, so deeply. We just accept it on faith, given the wide critical and popular acclaim that she received over the many years of her professional life, that independence was her core attribute. Deirdre Towers, a fellow dancer and writer wrote that "María Benítez is a quintessential American artist…who reflects a mix of cultural influences in her dance rhythm with all its primal drive and shifts…and displaying that elusive regal bearing of hers [that] suggests a pride in being an independent thinker."

When asked, María always reiterates that fire and passion are key elements for any flamenco dancer to possess, but she goes further by explaining that these things cannot be taught, you have to find them within yourself. She understood that the intelligence for dance was an inborn trait, and that finding a like intelligence in the audience would spark a wave of recognition

that could create a third form of intelligence, almost a visceral memory of what had transpired.

Although María received literally hundreds of rave reviews over her career, it is in the personal letters that she took the most pride, knowing that a connection had been made.

"Dear Maria,
I ushered for your show on the night that your mother was there in the audience and I just had to write this little note to tell you how moved I was by your dancing that night. I went home afterwards and could not sleep. You conjured up spirits and made magic happen. I feel lucky to have been there that night, I'm still inspired."

As previously mentioned, María understood the parallels between jazz and flamenco. In flamenco specifically, the song was at the core, "it came first." Then music was added, perhaps with guitar and percussion instruments, and it was only later that dance was added. And song of course was rooted in the beat. This was critical. As one of America's original art forms, jazz was deemed revolutionary given the context of racial oppression. Jazz is resistant to the rules of the dominant culture about how music should be written and performed. Resisting poverty and racism could be overtly employed as themes in the music, or simply performing it could be an act of resistance. This stance toward the dominant culture similarly applies to flamenco. María had the sly satisfaction of knowing that while the female form was being admired, she was sticking it to the man. While the quaint gypsy struggles of long-ago might not be relevant today, María was victim of double persecution—both Native and Spanish, so she knew how very critical protest was to the core purpose of dance. Given her gender, she had a rare triple

consciousness of what it meant to be an oppressed person.

María was inspired by both ancient musical forms and by contemporary ideas about art. She gives an example of her flamenco philosophy from a piece of her choreography: "In the course of my professional career, I work to extract core themes of Spanish dance and transport these ancient narratives into other dance forms through collaboration with innovative composers. This aspect of my choreography repertoire was based on composer Jordi Savall's historic work, *Folías de España*." La Folia is a traditional European musical theme, an eight-bar chord progression that has ancient links to peasant dances. Although many composers have used the harmonic theme and its melodies, Jordi Savall, a musician, conductor, and scholar of early European music, has interpreted la Folia in a unique blend of the traditional and the modern. Savall's musicians typically use traditional instruments, especially the viola family, but interpret the themes in a somewhat improvisational style.

In 2003, María choreographed three Folia pieces for Savall at the Joyce Theater in New York. Notes on that performance indicate the scope of María's vision: "She wants to push the boundaries of dance vernacular by continuing her exploration of this music through the fusion of ballet, Spanish dance, flamenco, and elements of modern dance." In flamenco, a hammer and anvil provide the rhythm for some of the oldest dances. María took this element and transformed it with Savall's Folia interpretations into a mix of old and new: "She envisioned incorporating a neo-classical set design centered around the prop element of the anvil: a set piece simultaneously obsolete and post-modern in its applications to the beat of contemporary life. Although María was not lending her voice to the culture by describing how her art could be viewed as an act of defiance, she was, nonetheless, lending her spirit to a cause. Her form of activism was to drill down to the core meaning of dance, and to make sure that her interpretation affected viewers strongly.

Some dancers keep emotion in check internally, and some let it out. María found a rare balance between these two extremes. She could appear to be waging an internal battle with a vortex of feeling, but the sensation of that inner world could escape the unseen and become palpable. Her key to the vortex was the intersection of beauty and meaning, albeit a transitory and fleeting one. Her methods to convey meaning were mysterious, a kind of lay ministry between the human and the divine. Argentine writer Jorge Luis Borges gives an argument for the existence of God that is akin to María's essence: If you witness a flock of birds, recalling the act of that sighting is inherently ambiguous and yet crystal clear because you will remember that you saw a number between one and ten, even if the exact number is elusive. Borges' thesis is that this memory of the flight of birds proves God's existence because the actual number cannot be indefinite, it must have taken place in an exact count. This transmutation of the indefinite and the transitory into the immutable and universal was María's inner logic as well. She might have no use to label and identify a feeling, for how do you begin to name something that is so powerful and yet so fleeting? To name it before you even experience it will already be too late. It is something that you will never see again, and will never be able to completely describe, yet all the same, it took your heart with it on the wind. This was how María felt about her audience. "I will dance for myself,

but perhaps you will join me for the experience, and afterwards, we will both secretly know what was shared." If, after a performance, the spirit moved you, then thunder had spoken and found words. The flamenco ensemble had made a way for the emotion to well up in you somehow, either through the feet of the dancer, the expression of the guitarist, or the voice of the *cantaor*. María used her performance to both hide and reveal her principles. To watch the intensity of her emotions, first hidden, then coming to the fore, was a feeling that was almost dizzying, a sense the center might not hold, that it all might self-destruct. That was the thrill, that paradoxical center spiraling almost out of control.

There are many traditional flamenco styles—the female solo, or *solea*, fast-paced *bulerías*—are just two examples, but María did not want to just explicate a type or a form. She wanted to make her performance the entirety of what you took away. This made her a risk taker in the extreme because critical reviews could pin the entire success or failure of a performance on her star power alone. She had to achieve this by refusing to be typecast. By being different. The set roles of maiden, seductress, or jezebel could be distorted by her artistry so that she could be all of those things yet none of them at the same time. She was something of an alien herself, always closed off from a true sense of belonging. Some naturalized citizens describe how a return to the mother country after achieving US citizenship, brings back an immediate form of recognition as if they had never left home. In contrast, others report the opposite effect in which they sense that the change in allegiance means that a return to the mother country is an act of betrayal that will permanently sever their ties to their former home, making their return to a place of origin conspicuous in the sense that former friends and neighbors see their otherness, and close the door to a meaningful return. María seemed cut off from

her former homes in this way.

As we know, María didn't want to trade on her beauty, but she certainly knew that there was power in being pretty and provocative. While she had no interest in becoming a fashion model or endorsing perfume, she knew that beauty didn't hurt as long as you were noticed for your artistic statement. She sometimes had to use beauty for greater ends, but she preferred to distort it or obscure it, and that in turn gave her an otherworldliness. This showed up in her indifference for use of the fan. The implied coquettishness of the fan did not suit her. Fans can also seem childlike, for the game of now-you-see-me, now-you-don't. In contrast, María was complicated and adult. She was deep and dark and profound, not light and airy and flirty. She wanted to keep a certain composure that could not be shaken, that kept her in a position of power like a warrior. As Santa Fé author Ana Pacheco described María's walking down the street, it was "moving like Athena" — complete with did invisible armor, shield, and plate around and about her.

María had a similar distaste for the veil. Playing the virginal bride was to her the worst, most boring role. Additionally, a veil can be opaque or obscuring. Even if a veil is clear or translucent, it can overpower the viewer with reflective light, obscuring the wearer. María wanted to be the one beaming at you, not her clothing. She wanted to be the source of the power and the light. Not a female moon but a masculine sun, at the center, all powerful. Castanets, in contrast, could pierce the dark, beat the anvil of time. María's disdain for the flamenco props of fan and flower can also be traced to the fact that she eschewed the fetish allure of dancers who projected a sexual aura. Although she was extremely seductive in her own way, she wanted to be strange and foreign and powerful. She reveled in the form of exotic that was more of a spell, where you made the discovery that you had been captured without your even knowing it.

María was always stalking the invisible fire at the center of the stage. Although a literal fire was seldom called for as part of the stage props, she could somehow conjure the fire's presence. This fire grew voraciously in the center, informing all of the dance. A campfire can be a symbol of many things: an exciting romantic adventure, a portent of impending doom, an incitement to anger, or perhaps contentment or new hope after the cold of winter or disappointment. Fire also defines space: strangers may not cross. In sensing that flames flickered in the center of the stage, viewers knew that the performers were all transfixed, mesmerized by the fire's terrible power. Somehow the audience felt that the blaze had been burning since time immemorial, taken by torch from campfire to campfire, always kept alive. Even if you didn't know who had set it, you understood why it was set and what it meant and how important it was to keep it going. The fire of flamenco carries more than momentary passion; the crimes and their victims of the past speak through the embers, and the play of light and dark in the flames brings both confession and recanting. There is anger, but anger with a purpose, to fight injustice. And if words could not be said aloud for fear of retribution, then the dance carried the message: that you must stand up, stomp your foot, cry out your heart, and leave the cloak on the floor, shredded to pieces. If that message was lost at times, then the false charm of the pretty face might taunt you, but the mystery of the flamenco and its morality play would remain.

Dance has at times in history been viewed as an act of rebellion, defying constraints. If this is true, it is even more true for flamenco, carrying with it, as it often does, subversive plans for rebellion or defiance. The dance in the opera *Carmen* is something of an act of rebellion by the cigarette girls. So dance choreography in flamenco is not just stamping and swirling; it carries a wealth of meaning about social class, caste, identity, and loss. María always stood in that power: to stand in her voice and to stand for something. She knew that you could rise above disenfranchisement. Native Americans were not guaranteed the right to vote in every state until 1962, despite the citizenship act of 1924. María knew that even though men she knew had gone off to fight in World War II, they came home to literal disenfranchisement. This was certainly one of the through-lines of her dance meaning: that dance was a defiant act. A teaching moment. A principled stand. Activism that taught that you could rise up, rise above any injustice that was holding you back. She taught rebellion in her movements and her demeanor and in her swagger.

In New Mexico, virtually everything is defined by the mountains. Natives followed the track of deer and bear through the mountains as the animals migrated. For invaders, the mountains were sign-posts to navigate their raids or conquests, and the Spanish settlers used mountains, valleys, and streams as markers for the land grants that families believed would establish their dynasties. But the landscape is also defined by marks from other pasts. The moon once kissed a huge sea in much of what is now New Mexico, and strange rock formations left behind by centuries of erosion still cast strange shadows. Volcanic eruptions left a landscape with alien scars in El Malpais and the Bisti Badlands. The dominance of the land and of its history sets New Mexicans apart from other Americans in what they value. An old pickup truck and two goats may enough to be a ranch, if the sense of the land is strong enough. For María, it was a pivotal moment when she realized that she could shape her career on that sense of the past. She could revel in her extraordinariness because what might make you an outcast in mainstream America could make you a celebrity in terms of the New Mexico heritage, a sort of reverse colonization that could invert the role of the past into the present. María's Spanish half was at once royal and outcast, a dual polarity meaning that she had to balance the needs of her own self with the expectations of her flamenco audience. In contemporary American culture, both the heirs of Native North America and the descendants of Spanish kings and queens were dispossessed of their regal stature, but María defied any attempt to constrain her to a predetermined fate.

María was always struggling to balance the needs of her self, the needs of her audience, the commands of the director, the whims of the marketplace, and the demand of the ultimate truth at stake. Struggle was embodied in the cultural shape of the dance itself. As we have said, in the communal aspect of Native American dance, there is no exceptionalism, no "star" of the dance. Similarly, in Native culture, the spiritual thinking does not recognize an individual's "soul" as a central entity to be saved. In contrast, in Spanish Catholic culture, the soul is everything, and in flamenco, the soul is the center, the essence of a dancer putting forth the self. María's soul did stand out, but in a shared or communal fashion. She felt your pain. Lived your lie and fought your battle. By turning around these concepts and exploring what it all meant, María stood for the idea that all dance kept to the same beat. We are all identical. Ultimately, even if externally she appeared as a diva or a prima, she contrasted that with the broadcast of her emotion as universal and of the people.

It was in this fashion that María was essentially dancing the map of New Mexico, re-living its terrible history of genocide and oppression while observing its competing cultures. She could skirt that line between offending the viewer and including them in her expression. She always knew where that line was drawn, even if sometimes, for political expediency, she would choose to obey convention and disregard the conflict that she knew was inherent in the face of the map of the land and its people. She knew that flamenco is a map of the world and a record of the history of the world.

In New Mexico, place names are Native, Spanish, and English, marking the history of the region. A common theme is the enchantment of the area. Place names reveal this way of describing the state, like "Golden," "Turquoise Trail," "Angel Fire," or "Enchanted Circle." Even if there is misery or poverty, the place names evoke love and lightness, similarly apt for flamenco themes. Although pain may always be afoot, love is the air between the dancers, especially so for the female. She may be the reviled gypsy thief or a courtesan fighting to survive; a shunned or fallen woman; a terrible beauty—but she is the one woman that you want in your corner.

It was in *El Amor Brujo* (sometimes translated as "Wedded by Witchcraft") that María found a role perfectly suited to her aesthetic. The classic piece by Manuel de Falla is literally about a magician and spell-bound love. Alongside mezzo-soprano Denyce Graves, María's performance was featured nationally on the PBS "Evening at Pops" series. Notably, considering the theory of flamenco and jazz as sharing an artistic impetus, jazz musician Miles Davis recorded in

1960 a section of *El Amor Brujo* entitled "*Canción del Fuego Fatuo*" ("Song of the will-ò-the-wisp").

This theme of bewitched love is fitting for the land of enchantment that is New Mexico. Places in the region carry a sense of strange dichotomy or paradoxical opposition. A monolithic image of a pueblo on a postcard presents a silent, mysterious façade to the world, but inside those walls a culture exists at odds with Hollywood clichés. Santa Fé also presents a façade of plain earthen walls, but wealth and glitter may

lie on the other side. And the thick adobe walls of a church in northern New Mexico may hide artworks whose traditions trace back to medieval times. Ancient petroglyphs etched in rock speak of ancient worlds, scattered by time. María knew that this sense of mystery could enable masterwork: she could thrillingly depict a surreal journey into the dark recesses of the past, a dream-walk through the Conquest of New Spain, the Pueblo Revolt, and the societal upheavals brought about by the waves of cultures fighting for control of the mountains and the high desert plateaus. She knew, too, that this history

of violence and death set against depictions of hell and a bloody Christ on the Cross (the mountains around Santa Fé are called "*Sangre de Cristo*"), brought with it Catholic echoes of life, death, and afterlife— the core themes and grand stories of opera and flamenco. María was subversively suggesting the Native belief that the persona is not a soul belonging to a god. She was a wandering spirit, not a soul or a girl or someone who is owned by a man.

That sense of a wandering spirit is a metaphor for María's life. New Mexico has plazas or village centers in both Native and Hispanic communities. In the Pueblo, the space is sacred, where spiritual events are centered; in the Hispanic plaza, the events are more often celebratory or festive. María took them both and traveled effortlessly between worlds. The core lesson she somehow intuited from a Pueblo to which she never belonged was this: in ceremony begins understanding. Repetition and the coordination of body and spirit lead to the deepest level of initiation. In the Pueblo, a space is held open in the center, a place where certain needs are met, where stories unfold and are gathered up again. Dancing in this space held by the community is the most precious act, an act with a sense of permanence despite its fleeting nature. Similarly, María seemed to haunt the stage even when she had left it behind or when she waited the wings for the next act. The viewer felt her presence still.

The kind of dance that was María's calling was an act of bravery. Like Georgia O'Keeffe defying her male peers and painting as she saw fit, María did as she pleased. She was recording the story of her self. She staged her life in a choreography that may have seemed a spontaneous adaptation, but was actually very deliberate. María took the space even if it was not all technically hers. The classic flamenco stage setup is the row of high-backed chairs along a back wall or a diagonal, with the spotlight on the *cantaor* or the row of guitars. The dancers occupy the stage as if circling a fire, their *chaîné* turns each time bringing fire-lit eyes back to the circle. The men and women come and go, they clash together, they melt together as the nebula of skirts and flying fringe cut across the space. And María alone transcends: she rises like a great black drape across a giant bowl of sky, drawing darkness in veils across mesa and mountain, cutting off the secondary dancers from view or bringing the singer's plaint in sharp focus, revealing, obscuring, a terrible drape of sadness. Veils can obscure both beauty and flaws; every visage may have a good side and an opposite bad side. María's geometry of dance underscored her ability to dissect angles, rotate around her own center, and cut through the algebra of the past. Despite the credits due to composer, lyricist, singer, accompaniment, and other principals, a performance could become known as hers and her alone.

The final component of María's legend was the *duende*, the deep sense that you knew that some spirit possessed you. The antecedents to "*duende*" refer to a spirit in Spanish and Portuguese folklore that literally means "goblin" or "ghost." If you had this type of spirit within, you could experience a heightened state of emotion that could conjure up the goblin-like magic creatures of Iberian mythology. This emotion cannot be manufactured or feigned. Having *duende* sets you apart, a separation that means you are

alone. But being alone could also mean that you could cast the biggest, most noticeable shadows. María chose to put forth her spirit, herself, so that even though part of her existence was just the fringe, she found other strands to weave together in a spiral whose center was her belief that sheer strength was what would determine her future, and that the weak had to be parted away and cast aside. The center will hold.

The library of María's movements showed this spirit, this *duende*, as the central drama of her character. She refused to be the feminine chalice waiting for her man, waiting for her receptacle to be filled with male god-spark. She wanted to be an independent player on the stage, the singular María even if she danced with a male dancer. Her dance movements were like the thrust and parry of fencing where, even though you fight the other person, the combination of the two sets of movements forms a third movement for the viewer. And it was a fight to the finish: the wounds seemed real and the blade switched the flesh. María presented the face of beauty, but darkness could seem to well up in her eye sockets, and the bloom of bruising seemed to spread, almost like a stigmata, an intimate connection between life, death, and resurrection. But then with lights on after performance, she was back to her self. A magician in a way. And also a con artist.

But it was a good con. Artists can become to be so closely identified with the art form that just hearing the music can trigger the recollection of the dance and the physical manifestations of being enthralled by it. María's art was her self.

CHAPTER FIVE - FORTH AND BACK

SIGUIRIYA (circa 18th century)

Cuando yo me muera,	When I come to die,
Te pío un encargo	I ask of you one favor,
Que con las trenzas de	That with the braids of
Tu pelo negro	Your black hair
Me mare las manos.	They tie my hands.

The plaintive form of singing in flamenco is not unlike some songs from many an ancient temple. It is as if a curtain is lifted on access to a sacred space. In that vision of a different place, the singer can evoke an amazing world that the exceptionally gifted inhabit. These extraordinary individuals seem like gods to their public—moving us, transporting us to beautiful realms so beyond and above ordinary earthly existence—but somehow bridging the divide between realms. For all the extraordinary amount of energy expended to perform, inspire, and transport, these rare artists can communicate deeply with us about their mundane human experiences in ordinary speech as well. That kind of humility is so

true of María, who loved to laugh and gossip and sit with a glass of strong red wine and a cigarette under the weeping cherry tree by the fountain within the adobe walls of her Santa Fé home, a home that she and Cecilio had christened *"La Piqueta"* after a bullring in Mexico.

To be successful in life, it helps to know where you are from. Through these pages, we have migrated from one point to another, finding María in the process. Individual images do not give the entire story, so it is now with the advantages of time and distance that we can stand back and see the entire mosaic of her life. For those toiling in the fringes of dominant society, or those who had to fight to persevere or assimilate, being treated unequally creates a constant state of opposition or cognitive dissonance that makes it hard to rest. While María always presented herself as perfectly composed, that persona masked a restless, boundless energy that may make her seem unable to find peace; she failed to find her place of repose. After retiring from the stage, and then from

teaching at her company, a void opened. The stage was where she belonged. Though trite to say, María was at one with the stage, and when she retired, an empty stage seemed symbolic of the void created by her absence. After so many decades of touring, leaving

her blood, sweat and tears onto the floors of stages everywhere, it is easy to imagine that her genetic material is in the very floorboards.

Some artists become so identified with their chosen art form that they are forever identified together. María and flamenco are synonymous. Additionally, María's spirit will linger long after she is gone because so many young dancers and established artists were taught by her or danced with or for her company. As she was quoted, asked about life after retirement from the stage, she responded, "I perpetuate. I disseminate. I train others." She has been blessed in her life with an internal mechanism that told her exactly what she needed to do in her career and when. For example, she knew at 14 or 15 years old that she did not have the temperament for ballet, that she needed to be free from its restrictions so that she could invent her own path. And when the time came to retire from the stage, she faced it forthrightly.

Dancing at the periphery of society means that you are on the fringe, but the advantage of being there is that you are not beholden to society's rules. María was on the fringe for so long that she became the center. She saw no boundaries. It was as if she were a centripetal force in the emotional arc of her own life, and that she drew everything into her orbit, incorporating what she wanted and discarding the rest. Even though she was between different worlds, she defiantly occupied all of that intervening space.

Even when exact details of María's performances defy memory, the impact remains, long after the stage goes dark. She left her stamp on New Mexico permanently like a lightning strike leaving a mark on the land. In remote Spanish communities, wood cutters search for trees hit by lightning because the resin is caramelized by fire, forming hard nuggets of resin-soaked wood called "*ocatito*" or "heart of the wood" which are prized out of the stumps for their value as fire starter.

María played a huge role in developing modern flamenco. Santa Fé and Albuquerque are now known as destination spots for a resurgence of this art form. The state's famous fusion of cultures and influences has taken something that began around gypsy campfires—and was performed in royal courts—and transformed it into an accessible and relatable art form which can still command the grand stages of the world. In schools, state legislative funding for flamenco lessons to fight childhood obesity has benefitted

hundreds if not thousands of students, and a new generation of audiences. The market for performance has been changed by María's long tenure at Santa Fé Fiesta and at Santa Fé's Spanish Market, with her "Next Gen" performances at the Plaza bandstand. Flamenco in New Mexico has exploded, with many professional companies based in Santa Fé and Albuquerque. Even if alliances María built should become frayed or competition drives some companies away, the performance scene has been permanently changed by her life's work.

María was entirely unique partly because she imbued standard movements with personal meaning. She could cut the sky with a power fist, or make her skirt slash darkness like a knife. While she was not a part of Taos Pueblo, she somehow understood the permanence of its traditions. Archeologists sometimes suppose that Native cultures are extinct and that excavating structures of the past will provide significant clues to understanding ancient peoples. However, in New Mexico, Native culture was not obliterated but lived on, going underground in order to survive extinction. Its secrets are not served by excavations and removals of patrimony. María understood this; she knew the iconography of Kachina culture in

Native communities was secret, that you did not have to explain it, and that it was improper to explain it. Thus, María could inhabit her own universe and allude to grand mysteries without having to parse the meaning. In her own way, María was a light among the ruins of history— flashing on the impenetrable without exposing it.

While María was not pursuing a scholarly interest in movements to undo the damage of the past and not asserting a grand artistic and historical reconciliation, her art nevertheless did much to bridge cultural and social divides. She was not a peacemaker between warring cultures. She was not trying to heal human culture. But by keeping her composure and embodying cultural differences, she helped, indirectly, to highlight and interpret the battle. María seemed to be making an artistic statement that the viewer and the dancer should not simply revel in the beauty of flamenco. Rather, she was saying that by distorting dance conventions to show our true "otherness" to one another, that would be the actual beauty of the dance, because in the end our uniqueness is the only authentic thing that we possess.

María did not want to occlude the truth. Bonds of privation and struggle in the vast wilderness of New Mexico are not a sufficient basis for a unified people. The past wars still percolate to this day and cannot be simply ignored; history must be examined and resolved. She did not want to take things out of sight of reality. She shunned the virginal opaqueness of veils that hide beauty and hint at purity until the big reveal at the altar. She would don a veil if the composition or the director called for it, but she wore it more to suggest the duality of concealing and revealing. She didn't smile from behind a fan, but held it more as a weapon, always at the ready if needed for thrust and parry. She termed what she did Spanish "art," not just dance. She knew that the integrity of the cultures behind the art demanded truth. Her nonprofit, formed with her husband Cecilio, was the "Institute for Spanish Arts" because she knew that preserving culture was vitally important in the face of American homogeneity and commercialism. The Institute had to function as a school, not solely a space for entertainment. She understood the global issue that education had to be a force for both societal change and cultural preservation. This view took the role of art and culture seriously, not just an idle dance of flirtatious women. In the opera *Carmen*, the factory girls who dance alongside the title-role singer take on a sort of group character, *en masse*. They stand for the fight against the class system and economic privation, the struggle against the powerful. The simple gypsy flourish, stomp, and swirl were in some sense a distraction under which a political message could be smuggled into the opera's story. By always retaining her composure on stage, María could be serious about the message. She knew that the side roles or bit parts could influence thinking, not just cheer on the title singers.

Filmmaker Merrill Brockway's retrospective movie in 2007 about María, *María Benítez: Yesterday, Today, and Tomorrow* is a perfect title for a film based in a state so steeped in history. For anyone with a strong sense of the past, yesterday is always somehow present, and tomorrow is informed by the past as well. María had an eternal quality that was neither traditional nor transitory. She could occupy all of her art's allotted roles— maiden, enchantress, goddess, hag, witch, sage, ghost— simultaneously. She knew how to convey great emotion in her art, perhaps because she understood the sadness of the past. Great sadness finally came and sat by her side with the loss of her husband and her parents. With health challenges and the dormant Institute, she was struck by the realization that her legacy would largely be seen through the lens of the great successes of her former students. This would prove to be one of her greatest roles, being the "*madre*" for other instructors and schools that employ her methods.

There are countless videos of María's performances, but she lives most strongly in our memories of those performances, in the intangible ways that our lives and our culture was changed. Each memory of her performance is a jewel of feeling that can never be, or never was, but which still somehow persists. Turquoise, the state gem, is an apt metaphor for her influence. Turquoise is formed when water seeps through stone with a high mineral content. It is usually formed in dry landscapes, often in crevices of volcanic rock, or thrown from a volcanic eruption. Similarly, María's influence shows a unique cultural transformation against the state's often violent background of history. Extraction of turquoise can be a difficult process, and it is often hard to find. She was likewise rough and defiant; she knew she was in the in-between place, hidden in plain sight by a culture that lauded cheerleaders and ballroom dance and mainstream music before flamenco was even a blip on the popular culture's radar. María knew that her artistry was not only completely outside mainstream culture but was also never fully intersected with any single part of New Mexican culture. It wasn't fully Spanish. It wasn't fully Native. However, it was in this in-between place where she found her strength. It gave her a sort of otherworldliness in the sense that she was all-powerful, that she could control the elements, and that she answered to no one artistically. Her entire life is the archetypal flamenco metaphor: fighting the system, escaping confines, defying expectations in ways that meant that she could feel deeper and love more intensely than anyone else. María knew that she had to be fought for, that she might accept a great love only to rebuff it and toss it aside, and that a fight with a bull may end in death. María could convey all these feelings because she knew what discrimination felt like. She had experienced the classic emotions of the flamenco story: always being the "other," always being on the outside, on the outskirts, never in the center. Because her life began in the fringe or on the outskirts, she was able to position herself in the dead center in the key dramas of human existence. She refused to be sidelined as an exotic attraction. She refused to be an ordinary member of the cast; she chose instead to be deployed like a raging torrent, to sweep away the past and cut a new way for the future. She was like lightning that is destructive and beneficial, bringing rain. She created a legacy in her compositions, her training methods, her choreography, and the community that built up around the dance. The *cantaor,* the *guitarrista,* and the dancers on her stage seemed like a tiny band of fighters deep in the woods, stoking the fire of rebellion far from prying eyes, singing their song to the skies, fading in and out with the wind, and minding no one. This was no tribe but her own. She inhabited the role of a great figure striding across the mythical New Mexican landscape, taking the stage as her own. She knew that each succeeding culture had claimed the region: the state had been ruled by the Indigenous people, the Spanish, the Mexicans, and finally the Americans, but the sense of people and place was immutable. She was all New Mexican, not through birthright but through her profound connection with the state's story and her adoption of its mythology. In that process, she gained a mythic stature of her own.

CIRCLING BACK
A Note from the Author

I grew up in the era when young girls confided their thoughts to little diaries that were constructed with a locking flap that could be opened with a tiny and mostly useless key. Girls would pour out their innermost thoughts without realizing that future yard sales and dumpster divers could someday expose those very personal confessions to the entire world. While these youthful ramblings were mostly confined to juvenile drama and battles with self-doubt, adults also populated the pages. Mostly parents. Sometimes teachers.

In my dog-eared journal, famed flamenco dancer María Benítez leapt off the page. She was larger than life, and in typical youthful fashion, the letters of her name were decorated with daisies and stars. This famous luminary had graced the stages at El Nido and The Santa Fe Opera. She had toured around the world. But she was also my dance teacher. At Acequia Madre Elementary School in those days, after-school activities were not as highly regulated as they are today. Roving bands of kids wandered the neighborhoods, doing all the things that today would land the parents in trouble with officials from the Children, Youth and Families Department. We were trouble-makers, in an innocent sort of way. We stole apples from the fields around Canyon Road. We played in the irrigation ditches. We made so much noise in Cathedral Park once that a tired Monsignor came out and gave us a lecture filled with fire and brimstone. We knew which houses would have fresh tortillas after school, and who owned a color television set. We knew how to buy just one piece of bologna at Tito's Food Line, or penny candy from Gormley's. The only time I wasn't running amok was when I was taking ballet classes under Louise Licklider's tutelage at the rambling adobe dance hall on Camino del Monte Sol, across from the mysterious Union Protectiva building. Louise used the Russian method, meaning she deployed a thin bamboo cane—more of a switch, really—to whip our lazy backs into straightness. When she told us to bend over to form a stiff ironing board shape, the cane was busy flicking around the room to ensure the proper technique. Part of our instruction was learning Spanish dance and castanets from María, and her grace and beauty served as a luminous counterpoint to the sharp wrath of ballet and toe shoes.

I was petrified of Mrs. Licklider. When my parents would bump into "Louise" on the plaza, her huge bun of red hair was undone, and the hair reached to her knees. She betrayed no clue to my parents that she was a stern taskmaster, and one Fiesta occasion, she sported a fancy mahogany cane with a hidden screw top well, presumably for some kind of punch which I later found out was an adult beverage.

When Licklider announced her production of *The Nutcracker Ballet*, it was the social event of the season at the elegant Greer Garson Theatre on the campus of the College of Santa Fe, with María Benítez, of course, cast as "Spanish Chocolate" in the production. But my tiny part in the Children's Scene posed a huge challenge. Whether due to anxiety or age-related developmental delay, I simply could not remember the steps. Even the bamboo whip could not cure my slow-wittedness. Afraid that I would be a huge embarrassment to the entire production, I begged my parents to create some sort of excuse for me, but they laughed and commented about ballet being the equivalent of military school for girls. Riding horses with the Annon kids, I fantasized about leaping off my horse and breaking an ankle, thereby rescued from the shame and

humiliation of dancing with my classmates. Knowing the intensity of ballet training in general, and Licklider's stern methods in particular, I have insight now for how these rigors must have been part of María's core.

After my mother passed away, my father could no longer afford dance classes. I certainly did not have any talent, but word of a scholarship came through, with my benefactor being none other than María Benítez.

Somehow the Santa Fé of that era was a close-knit web of togetherness. A kid whose family couldn't pay for necessities could still get what she needed, no questions asked. There was no premium "Eastside" of the city; millionaires lived next door to blue-collar people. Homes on the Eastside were not considered better than or more expensive than other homes because everything was made out of dirt. Celebrities mingled seamlessly with everyday folk. In my case, my diary entries reflect that my family was blessed to meet dancer Jorjé Midón up in Dixon at Robert and Carolyn Grant's house perched near an irrigation ditch. Children of famous actors attended my elementary school, Acequia Madre, sharing cooties with the children of cops and waitresses. I envied the kids with *manteca* (lard) spread on a tortilla, more so than the kids with Wonderbread and jelly. My mother baked a molasses concoction into brown bread, using old coffee cans instead of baking pans. Having New Mexico as our emergence story was a sacred blessing. A birthright unparalleled. Out of the cholla and ragweed, a little girl could traverse the world.

The kindness paid to me in the form of a scholarship that allowed me to continue to be part of the community—despite my woeful lack of talent—was what made María a giant in my little diary. While precious stories of childhood are ultimately discarded and forgotten, some figures are never lost to us. We take them to the end. In my personal landscape of New Mexico, María is that solitary volcanic landmark highlighted by a single bolt of light—veiled in clouds but puncturing the sky with an outstretched arm—casting all the mountains around her into shadow.

—Jaima Chevalier

PHOTO EDITOR STATEMENT

The photographic record of María's life and career is astounding. The wealth of material is staggering, and choosing selections for this book was extremely difficult, especially given María's riveting image. Collection of the images took years, and because we did not in all cases have complete access to the records of María's organizations, we created a new collection from a huge range of sources: professional photographers, amateurs, museums, archives, private collections, and so on. Once collected, the images posed various challenges for reproduction in this book. Each photograph contains history not only of the subject, but also of the times and the particular image maker. For example, photographers of yesteryear, working with film, were forced to choose between speed (to capture María's blistering-fast movements) or light (to capture her beauty and character). Additionally, red was a difficult color to capture, and that tint in some of these photos creates a vintage glow that we chose in some cases, not to color-correct. Flamenco performances are often held in dimly-lit spaces, so use of existing light was a major challenge, forcing the photographer to push technology to the limits. In every case, however, miracles were captured, and we are proud to present this sub-set of images that portray a true icon in all her glory.

—Brian Fishbine

FOR FURTHER READING

Afanador, Ruven. *Mil Besos.* 2014.
Chávez, Nicolasa. *The Spirit of Flamenco.* 2015.
Edwards, Gwynne with photography by Haas, Ken. *¡Flamenco!* 2000.
Ortiz Vásquez, Dora. *Enchanted Temples of Taos.* 1975.
John, Suki. *Contemporary Dance in Cuba, Técnica Cubana as Revolutionary Movement.* 2012
Tallchief, Maria. With Larry Kaplan. *Maria Tallchief / America's Prima Ballerina.* 1997

CREDITS

Cover Image, Ruven Afanador

Dance Magazine images, Jack Mitchell, page 2

Dancing couple, photographer unknown, page 3

Early New Mexico performance, Tony Vinelli, page 3

Pat Goudvis, page 4

Beverly Gile, page 6

Family photographs, courtesy María, page 10

BG Randall photographs, c.1905, postcards by (c) Las Quince Letras 1986-87, pages 11,12, 13

Kiva photograph, private collection, page 13

Courtesy María, page 14

Joseph Amadeus Fleck, *Talpa Valley*, courtesy image, page 14

María dancing during the Fiesta de Taos, courtesy María, page 15

Taos News article, 1958, page 16

María's childhood pictures, courtesy María, page 17

Images left to right, top row: Peggo Cromer, photographer unknown, Peggo Cromer, page 18

Images left to right, bottom row: Brian Fishbine, Elsa Kendall, (c) Don J. Usner, page 18

Knifewing photograph, courtesy the author, page 19

Eagle dancers at Museum of Indian Arts and Culture, Brian Fishbine, page 20

Black Mesa and chapel, Brian Fishbine, page 21

Martha of Taos postcards circa 1955-1965, page 22

Images of Pop Chalee by Charles E. Lord, courtesy Tony E. Martinez, page 23

Taos from Above, courtesy Chris Dahl-Bredine @shotsfromabove, page 24

María Invades Spain, Atencio Studio, page 26

María's First Photo Shoot, Atencio Studio images (3), page 27

First Marquee, photographer unknown, page 28

Ken Holland photograph, page 28

Madrid newspaper, page 29

Singer Luis Vargas in front of the Wilshire Ebell Theatre, early 1980s, page 30

Marquee, photographer unknown, page 30

Louise Licklider Studio portrait (top left), page 31

María aloft, photograph by B.B. Lopez (top middle), page 31

New Mexico Magazine, July/August 1970 (top right), page 31

Courtesy, private collector, photographer unknown, page 32

PHOTO GALLERY, Images Ruven Afanador, Ken Howard, Beverly Gile, Winter Prather images courtesy Winter Prather Collection (Ph.00332, History Colorado), Jack Mitchell, Brian Fishbine

Pat Goudvis, page 119

Marilyn Foss image of Cecilia and María Benítez, mid-1980s, page 119

Randall West (c) 2002, page 120

Dallas Opera's 2004 production of *El Amor Brujo,* María with singer Denyce Graves, photographer unknown, page 121

Robin Holland superimposed images, page 121

Actor Larry Hagman autographed poster, page 122

Artist images (3) by Marianne Cobbett, early 1980s, page 122

Artist image by Marianne Cobbett (upper left), page 123

Sketches (upper middle and upper right) by artist J. Cooke, 1995, page 123

Robin Holland image of María choreography, 1989, page 123

María with Vicente Romero, 1970, photo courtesy Lili del Castillo and Luís Campos, page 124

María in floral dress, photograph by Tony Vinelli, page 125

Pat Goudvis image of María with shawl at El Gauncho summer season, late 70s-early 80s, page 125

"Whirling dervish" superimposed images, photographer unknown, page 126

Winter Prather image of María's back, courtesy Winter Prather Collection (Ph.00332, History Colorado), page 127

Boots on tour, uncredited, page 127

Tone Stockenström images (3), page 128

White pants take the floor, El Nido 1974, photographer unknown, page 128

The company, photograph attributed to James B. Russell, page 128

Lois Greenfield images (2), page 129

Estampa Flamenco, photographer unknown, page 132

Morgan Smith images (3), page 130

Tony Vinelli images, pages 131-132

Len Prince image, page 134

María's student "Gio," photo by the author, page 139

Beverly Giles, page 142

"La Piqueta" image by the author, page 143

Morgan Smith image, page 144

María's teacher portrait, page 147

The Black Swan, Louise Licklider, page 148

Licklider Studio images, with María, page 148

María in the mirror, Sergio Oddo, page 154

Back Cover Image, Winter Prather Collection (Ph.00332), History Colorado

Collage by
Jo Ann Garcia Orellana

Asked for romantic stories about being a gypsy dancer on the road, Benítez rolls her dark eyes heavenward. "It was exciting to be a teenager in Spain and to have a job dancing. But it's a hard and unglamorous life. I wish I had a peseta for every hour I've spent kneeling over a bathtub of cold water to wash my costume in the middle of the night. There must be thirty yards of cloth in the *bata de cola* with a six-foot train and all those flounces. You have to wash it every day because the thing has to be starched and ironed. We danced in bullrings. Our dressing rooms were the bull stalls, with a curtain or two thrown up for decency's sake. If you wanted hot water to wash off your makeup you had to carry your own immersion heater. Then immediately after the performance we'd travel to the next town and have to find our own lodgings for the night. There was just a lot of plain knocking about."

—Daniel David.
"Vogue Arts/Dance." *Vogue*, July 1991, pp. 82-84.

Made in the USA
San Bernardino, CA
11 June 2019